DESIGN AND INTENT
IN
AFRICAN LITERATURE

Edited By

David F. Dorsey
Phanuel A. Egejuru
Stephen H. Arnold

ANNUAL SELECTED PAPERS OF THE ALA
5/1979
Series Editor:
Stephen H. Arnold

The ALA acknowledges with great appreciation
the assistance rendered by the University of Alberta
in making publication of this book possible

"NKYIN KYIN"

Adinkra Symbol:
*"Changing oneself;
playing many roles"*

THESE PAPERS WERE SELECTED FROM THE 5TH ANNUAL MEETING OF THE AFRICAN
LITERATURE ASSOCIATION, MARCH 21-14, 1979, INDIANA UNIVERSITY, BLOOMING-
TON, INDIANA.

The ALA is an independent professional society founded in 1974. Membership is open to scholars,
teachers and writers from every country. The ALA exists primarily to facilitate the attempts of a
world-wide audience to appreciate the creative efforts of African writers and authors. The organization
welcomes the participation of all who produce the subject of our study. While we hope for a
constructive interaction between scholars and artists, the ALA as an organization recognizes the
primacy of African peoples in shaping the future of African literature.

The ALA publishes the quarterly *ALA Bulletin* for its members. Membership is for the calendar year
and available on the following terms (U.S. funds, 1982 rates): $12.00 regular members; $4.00 for
students, unemployed and retired; $18.00 for institutions; $25.00 and up for Sponsors. The ALA
publication office is % S.H. Arnold, ALA Editor and Secretary-Treasurer, Department of Comparative Literature, University of Alberta, Edmonton, Alberta, Canada T6G 2E6.

First Edition

Three Continents Press, Inc.
1346 Connecticut Avenue, N.W.
Washington, D.C. 20036

Cover Design by Tom Gladden

ISBN: 0-89410-354-7
ISBN: 0-89410-355-5 (Paperback)
LC No.: 82-50450

TABLE OF CONTENTS

Introduction   1

The South   5

The Ethics of an Anti-Jim Crow   7
Richard Rive

Out of the Garden   17
John Cooke

The North   29

A Feminist Critique of the Algerian Novel of French Expression   31
Mildred Mortimer

Taos Amrouche, Fabuliste   39
Claude Chauvigné

The East   49

A Basic Anatomy of East African Writing   51
Bernth Lindfors

Ng'ombe Akivundika Guu...: Preliminary Remarks on the
Proverb-Story in Written Swahili Literature   59
F.E.M.K. Senkoro

Techniques and Problems in Swahili Proverb Stories:
The Case of Baalawy   71
Carolyn A. Parker

The West   81

The Absence of the Passionate Love Theme in African Literature   83
Phanuel A. Egejuru

Independence and Disillusion in *Les Soleils des Indépendences*:
A New Approach   91
Fredric Michelman

Soyinka's *Season of Anomy*: Ofeyi's Quest   97
Obi Maduakor

The Child-Narrator and the Theme of Love in Mongo Beti's
    Le pauvre Christ de Bomba   103
    Abioseh Porter

Extra-Continental 109

The Use of African Literature in Anthropology Courses   111
    Nancy J. Schmidt

The West Indian Presence in the Works of Three New
    Central American Writers   119
    Ian I. Smart

Sarah Lee: the Woman Traveller and the Literature of Empire   133
    Susan Greenstein

INTRODUCTION

The annual conferences of the African Literature Association have regularly provided valuable scholarly and artistic experiences for those who attend. Each conference offers its own new and often unanticipated rewards. The meeting at Bloomington, Indiana, March 21-24, 1979 was notable for several reasons.

Through the kind financial support and cooperation of Crossroads Africa, the meeting was enriched by a delegation of francophone, anglophone and lusophone African authors, representing over twelve nations. In addition to their participation in panels and other sessions, there was the invaluable opportunity for informal discussions with these authors, some on their first visit to America.[1] A particularly salient instance of the chance for learning and inspiration from participating authors is the keynote address of Richard Rive (included in this volume, a moving account of personal experience and a testimony to the continued struggle for freedom and dignity for the oppressed masses of South Africa).

The 1979 Conference showed an encouraging increase in attention to three areas of our purview which are still under-represented in our courses and publications. They are: North African literature, diasporic literature, and above all, oral and written literature in indigenous African languages. This volume, therefore, more than any previous ALA Annual, is able to present analyses of individual works which reflect the geographical reality of African peoples and of people of African origins; it even presents one paper that examines novels of Africa written by a European.

A third feature of the Conference at Bloomington was a converging, though unorchestrated choice in method of approach in many papers presented. There emerged a prevalence of essays which focused on detailed study of particular texts and genres. The Conference bore no designated unifying theme, such as at Evanston, Illinois in 1976 (the Teaching of African literature), at Madison, Wisconsin in 1977 (Artist and Audience: African Literature as a Shared Experience), or at Gainesville, Florida in 1980 (Defining the African Aesthetic).[2]

---

[1] Members of the Crossroads Africa group included: Noureddine Aba (Algeria), Oumar Bâ (Mauritania,) Sylvain Bemba (People's Republic of the Congo), El Mubarak Bashier El Mubarak (Sudan), Lucien Lemoine (Senegal), Gérard Ake Loba (Ivory Coast) Robertson Mukuni (Zambia), Mathias N'gouandjika (Central African Republic), Sydney Onyeberechi (Nigeria), Titanga Pacere (Upper Volta), Peter Palangyo (Tanzania), Lenrie Peters (Gambia), Richard Rive (South Africa), Monganc Serote (South Africa). Other visiting authors included: Dennis Brutus, Peter Nazareth, Atukwei Okai, Amelia House, and Kofi Anyidoho. Our special thanks to Edward Brathwaite whose brief but inspiring "performance" set a cheerful stage for subsequent performances by other attending artists. His brilliant presentation of African cultural continuity in the New World did much to establish the Carribean presence in the conference.

[2] The proceedings of the first conference of the ALA, held in March 1975 at the University of Texas, Austin, were entirely devoted to South African literature. Bernth Lindfors edited them and they appear in *Issue*, volume 6, no. 1 (1976). The proceedings of the second conference, held in 1976 at Northwestern University in Evanston, Illinois, were edited by Thomas A. Hale and Richard Priebe: *The Teaching of African Literature* (Austin: University of Texas Press, 1977). In 1977, the ALA met at the University of Wisconsin, Madison; see Priebe, Richard K. and Thomas A. Hale, editors, *Artist and Audience: African Literature as a Shared Experience* (Washington, D.C.: Three Continents Press, 1979). The 1978 Annual, from the meetings at Appalachian State University in Boone, North Carolina, were edited under the title *When the Drumbeat Changes* by C.A. Parker, H. Wylie, A.M. Porter, and S.H. Arnold (Washington, D.C.: Three Continents Press, 1981). The 1980 volume, edited by B. Cailler, M. Hill-Lubin, R. Hamilton, and L. Johnson, is scheduled to appear in 1982 as *Defining the African Aesthetic*, also with Three Continents Press.

Therefore no special focus of subject or method influences the editors in selecting papers for this volume. Nevertheless, the Conference itself, as well as these essays, does suggest out title's emphasis on authorial purpose and design.

In selecting papers, the editors were severely limited by ALA funds; as a consequence several informative, interesting, stimulating discussions had to be excluded. The editors had to rely upon the literary quality and merit of individual essays, but mostly upon each paper's contribution to a deeper exploration and understanding of African literature.

As with any discipline concerning contemporary man, the study of African literature constantly evolves, constantly invents, refines, rejects or codifies an endless succession of concepts, methods, criteria. One encouraging experience in editing these papers was the indication of a concensus among the Association's members, committing themselves to principles of responsible, detailed and rigorous scholarship. Several such principles warrant comment here, not because they are nascent or dubitable, but because they do not always characterize studies of African literature, especially studies by those with limited direct experience of life on the continent. These principles may be categorized as matters of premise, of method, and or prupose.

Several *a priori* tenets have frequently distorted the perception of African literature. It is still occasionally necessary to assail the spurious criterion, "universality," which is supposed to invest all literature of serious worth. Universality is in fact more appropriately manifest in those readers whose sensibility can be attuned to the full diapason of human experience. Even more often, critics and analysts examine African literature with preconceived concepts of genres, their appropriate structures, artistic devices and subject matter. Sometimes laboriously gleaned data are rendered worthless by consignment to procrustean pigeon-holes. Preconceptions of the ethical or political stance appropraite to literary art (or to Africans) continue to deter accurate appreciation of the art before us. While every reader (and commentator) has a right and responsibility to define his or her own ethical demands, intellectual integrity requires the critic to distinguish his own from the author's and to identify and analyze the author's value system — *before* judging it.

But it is in method that studies of African literature now cover the widest spectrum of rigor and usefulness. In contrast to preconceptions of genre or allegiance to Euro-centric schools of literary analysis, our scholarship must demand induction rather than deduction and reduction as the primary approach to the analysis of texts. Every author, indeed every work, deserves to be seen as it is, whole, integral and unique, before one arrives at generalizations about its parts or about its relationship to any literary or cultural environment and traditions. It should not need to be stated that each critic who would commit his perceptions to print ought to be required to seek a familiarity with the historical, social and literary context of the work he discusses. The level of an alien critic's comprehension can never, of course, equal the author's. But a genuine impulse to academic precision is as clarion as conscience in calling a scholar to task when he ventures assertions unfounded in securely established fact. No one can be asked to know every remotely relevant fact. Everyone can be expected to recognize and be accountable for the limits of his information.

Criticism of African literature has tended in the past toward duplication of effort. When libraries are poorly stocked one expects to see the wheel invented over and over again, and for it to have flat sides on occasion. But the editors are pleased to report a erceptible shift away from tired, basic topics like ''tradition and modernity,'' and ''oral elements in the writing'' of a few well-known authors, and a move toward topics that demand research. And they are also glad to see more and more authors showing a command of previous scholarship relevant to their topics, scholarship often difficult to consult, not just because of poor libraries but because of an as yet weak bibliographic infrastructure to facilitate library travel through the areas we study.

A final criterion of reliable method, crucial to our field, then, is careful and adequate documentation. We all deal with the literature of many countries and cultures. We all must sometimes use the reports of others regarding literature in languages which we do not know. Our materials are printed on six continents by hundreds of presses, some flourishing, some ephemeral. Our sources are often oral only, or personal. For all these reasons the verifiability of statements and the practice of verification (both indispensable to authentic scholarship) are more difficult and more important than in many other fields of study. Therefore careful, complete and exhaustive documentation is an especially important feature of all serious commentary on African literature.

Aside from an inductive approach and an adequate source of information, all literature deserves well reasoned, perspicuous, cogent argumentation. Fuzzy cliched concepts, subjective, impressionistic observations hop-scotch plot summaries, and self-evident paraphrases do not well serve the present efflorescence of the continent's literature. The tight weave of fact with thought, and of explicit feeling with exact statement is essential for the validity, and hence the utility of any explication.

Along with examined premises and rigorous methods, scholarship of African literature requires a special conception of purpose. Revardless of the critic's own views of the relationship of literature to life, he perverts the objects of his study when he does not honor the creator's sense of purpose. The concensus of African authors is self-evident in the creative literature itself, and confirmed by innumerable statements of the artists: African literature is a committed literature, a consciously intended social force, a voice for living people with vital concerns. An incisive comprehension of each work itself, its very structure and meaning, requires a consciousness of its purpose, and of the significance of its very existence. For this reason, the world-wide appreciation of African literature is fostered by those studies which, no matter how narrowly focused on specific facets of specific works, suggest some significant inferences about literature or about literature in modern life. If *art for its own sake* has proven a Siren's call, then all the more destructive is criticism which ignores its own function as a social force.

In the editors' judgements, the papers in this volume exemplify these principles. The selection also demonstrates that these principles cast no undue limits on the variety of subjects, issues and approaches scholars may address or adopt. For example, Fikeni Senkoro's detailed study of formal structure in Swahili proverb-stories is not inconsonant with a clear exposition of their social function. We believe that each of these essays establishes a truth, a truth whose implications extend well beyond itself. Furthermore, the collection as a whole also demonstrates that, for a full understanding of a work of literature, the whole process of creation is relevant. A work's meaning is shaped by sources of inspiration (for fact and for form), by intentions of the author and his designs to attain them, by the interventions of editor, publisher and "the market," and even by the perceptions and evaluations of disparate audiences. Any work of art is a work of people acting in concert, and any who touch it, touch its meaning.

For the Conference itself, and for help with this volume, the African Literature Association is indebted to many individuals and institutions. The cooperation and patience of the authors were tried inordinately. Indiana University, Crossroads Africa, Emile Snyder as Conference Director and Karen Keim as his assistant were exemplary in producing a successful meeting. Jack D. Rollins, whose academic responsibilities in Africa required resignation as editor, was most instrumental in the initial collection of essays. A grant from the University of Alberta Faculty of Arts made possible the typing of the manuscript and helped defray other pre-publication costs.

DAVID DORSEY, Atlanta University
PHANUEL EGEJURU, Imo State University, Etiti Campus
STEPHEN ARNOLD, University of Alberta

THE SOUTH

THE ETHICS OF AN ANTI-JIM CROW

Richard Rive

Keynote address to the ALA Conference at the University of Indiana, Bloomington, Indiana: Friday, March 23, 1979.[1]

Firstly I must thank the organizers of the African Literature Association for the singular honour of inviting me to make this keynote address. I have no doubt that this is an honour intended primarily for those Black South African writers of the early 1950's like myself, who, amid repressions started pouring out their fledgling prose in Cape Town and Johannesburg, some of it derivative and attempting to resurrect Harlem in District Six and Sophiatown; some of it escapistic and concerning itself with Black guys and molls, boxers and football stars; and most of it angry and resentful, trying to shake an indifferent reading public out of its complacency and smugness.

I am going to start something a bit traumatic for me. This I have been shying away from for a long time. I am going to read the first, cautious beginnings of a selected study of my earlier life. If, as I understand it, the autobiography is structurally the marriage between history and the novel, then I might ask myself what claim to literature or sociology my own personal history has. I presume that the term *novel* here refers to form and shape rather than to treatment. Is my life then so unique that it warrants an autobiography? All lives are unique and so many millions of others in South Africa and other countries have shared a similar experience to mine. But these experiences are *unique* to me and to the way I respond to them and the way I articulate them.

My life story could take different shapes, for example the form of one of the many shattered South African Dreams. But then, is there anything left for any Black man's dreams, especially after Richard Wright exploded the myth of his realization of the American Dream? Can any black boy in South Africa ever dream of being accepted as a South African statesman, or doctor, or writer in his own country? Can any black boy in South Africa ever dream of being part of a meaningful law-making procedure in his own country? If any black boy does or did, it certainly never occurred to me and my ragged friends running wild in the mean streets of Cape Town's District Six. It never occurred to us that we were ever intended for anything other than what we saw surrounding us.

I was born in Caledon Street just below St. Marks Church which stood on windy Clifton Hill. I am using the past tense because Caledon Street has been wiped out. The streets in the District sloped down perilously towards the harbour so that our street was considerably higher than Hanover Street that ran parallel to it. Around us were the squalid, dark alleys, refuse-filled streets and mean lanes of Seven Steps, Horstley Street and Rotten Row. Under the Group Areas Act District Six has been reduced to rubble. Last year I was driving through the scarred landscape of what had been the scenes of my boyhood. Bloemhof Flats still stood,

---

[1] This address has also been published with the title "Caledon St. And Other Memories" in *Staffrider* (Nov.-Dec. 1979), pp. 46-49 and 61.

and St. Marks Church stretched solitary and defiant, and my stone-built primary
school lay in ruins, and the Fish Market and Star Bioscope were gone, and the
Globe Furnitures, where a vicious gang used to meet, had disappeared, and the
Swimming Baths and Maisels Bottle Store were no longer there. Where were the
crowded street-corners where we played around lamp posts in the evenings with
the South Easter howling around us? And where were the musty Indian stores
smelling of butterpits and spice? And the Fish and Chips Shop with sawdust on the
floor and the plate-glass windows steamed over with the heat from the boiling oil?
All these were gone because mean little men had seen fit to take our past away.

I remember that when I was three or four years old I ran away from out tenement
flat and wandered down Caledon Street determined to explore, but frightened stiff.
I stopped outside an impressive set of French doors which jutted out onto the
pavement. A red light burned in the window in spite of the bright morning sun. I
had stumbled on the most exclusive brothel on Caledon Street, run by a tyrannical
Madam called Mary *Worse*, or Mary Sausages. I think she received her nickname
because of her pronounced lips or pronounced buttocks or both. For a long time
she was the toughest, most generous and ugliest woman I had ever known. As I
paused outside her establishment one of the girls spotted me and enticed me inside
with a piece of candy. She was fair, I vaguely remember, with a rather worn, hard
face. She smiled and called out to the other girls that there was a new customer.
They all laughed and I could not understand this, so I began to cry and wanted to go
home. She lifted me up and set me down next to her. While she painted her
toe-nails I told her all about our family, how I could almost read, how my brother
Douglas went to a big school in de Villiers Street, how my mother could bake tarts
and yellow bread that had raisins in it. She listened attentively and then showed me
butterflies tattooed on her legs and warned me that they would fly away if one told
lies. I did not believe her because they still remained on her legs.

Mary Worse and the girls had a ritual every Christmas which I used to observe
for the many years while we lived in the District and I was a teenager. This
continued even after we had moved to Walmer Estate. Around 10 p.m. on
Christmas Eve all the customers would be put out unceremoniously from the
brothel, whether ill-dressed local thugs, or Chinese and Indian seamen, or well-
groomed respectable pillars of our local community who came surreptitiously, or
down-at-heel White pimps. The house was then closed for business, the curtains
opened up and the red light switched off. Mary and the girls would wash
themselves, put on fresh make-up and don their best dresses. Then, led by the
redoubtable Mary (whom rumour had it was a drum-major in the Girls Brigade in
younger and more innocent days), they would march up Caledon Street in double
file to attend midnight mass at St. Marks on the Hill. They would file self-
consciously into their seats and cry throughout the service, especially when they
felt that the references in the sermon were intended for them. By the time I was a
teenager and sang in the church choir on Sundays dressed in cassock, surplice and
Eton collar, the ritual was still going strong, and I would wink from our pews at
any of the girls I knew, and they would reciprocate with wan, tear-stained smiles.
After the Midnight service they would again fall into ranks outside the church and
march down the street, led by Mary. It was then open-house at the brothel for all

who cared to come. Everything was available except sex. The Rector of St. Marks was invited and put in a brief appearance. Wine flowed and there were plates heaped with chicken curry and yellow rice, boboties, jellies and custards, while the radiogram blared "O Come All Ye Faithful" and "Hark the Herald Angels Sing." By noon on Christmas it was all over. All the guests shook hands and left. The mess was cleared up and Mary and the girls went to bed and slept for the rest of the day. Later that evening they roused themselves, drew the curtain and switched on the red light. It was business as usual for the rest of the year.

It is notoriously simple to romanticize about slum life and write books sentimentalizing it. In truth the slum was damp, dirty and dank. As children we ran around bare-footed in patched clothes, howling at drunks and shouting obscene encouragement at bare-chested street fighters. Very rarely did the White World intrude into our area and when it did it was in the form of social workers bursting with compassion, or priests bursting with righteousness, or policemen strutting around in pairs and brazening it out with their hands always on their revolver holsters. There were also White liquor-runners and dagga-smugglers who were employed especially by shebeen-queens and brothel-owners.

I cannot find any reasonable objection to slum clearance, especially for the purpose of re-erecting decent living conditions for the former inhabitants. But when District Six was raised it was done by official decree to make room for those who already had more than enough. Today, almost two decades later, it has still not been built up. Those of us who had lived there before, people like Mrs. Barnes, and Mrs. Lewis and her daughters, and Honger, and Tana and Soelie Khan, were shifted out unceremoniously to the desolate, sandy wastes of Mannenberg and Heideveld, and a derelict area which with almost malicious sarcasm has been renamed Hanover Park. No White authority had ever bothered to ask me whether they could take my past away. They just brought in the bull-dozers. Dennis Brutus has written movingly about a similar situation four hundred miles away in Port Elizabeth, after the bulldozer had flattened South End.[2] When I went back last year I stood overlooking a wasteland on which weeds were growing, trying to reconstruct my childhood. I tried to estimate where our large tenement building, which housed twelve family units, had stood.

It was a huge, ugly, forbidding double-storeyed structure with a rickety, wooden balcony running its entire length. It contained three main entrances all of which faced Caledon Street. Behind it and much lower, running alongside it was a concrete enclosed area called the Big Yard into which all the inhabitants of the tenement threw their slops, refuse and dirty water. Below the street level, running under the building itself, was a warren of disused, gloomy rooms which were the remains of a Turkish Bath complex, a carry-over from the time when District Six was rich, white and Jewish.

The entrance to our section was numbered 201. The glass skylight above the door was pock-marked with holes my brother had shot into it with his pellet gun. After you negotiated the first flight of steps, which were of stone, you reached a wooden landing, where, as children, we would sit huddled in the artificial gloom,

[2] Dennis Brutus, "For them Burness Street is a familiar entity," in *Stubborn Hope* (Washington D.C.: Three Continents Press, 1978), pp. 23-24.

our thin jackets over our knees for warmth, and tell stories and fantasies about characters in the District. Two apartments ran off this floor, in one of which lived Mrs. Louw who had a pronounced Semitic nose, purpled by too much drinking. She was nicknamed Punch. Although well into her fifties it was rumoured that she had a boyfriend who was not only decades younger but was also White. In the other apartment lived Tant' Stienie, who was obese and vulgar, usually walked about bare-footed in a tight, dirty dress, and had half a dozen simian children from almost as many husbands. Up another flight of rickety steps, wooden this time, and you turned into pitch darkness. At the top of these steps was a tiny landing off which ran the two remaining apartments. One belonged to Aunt Becky and her husband. She had left her Dutch Reformed Mission Church because they were far too Afrikaans for her liking. Now she was a pillar of St. Marks. She also went to every Communist Party rally in the City Hall and dragged me with her. The other apartment belonged to our family, my mother, one sister, and three brothers. Another sister and two brothers were married and had already moved to Walmer Estate. The brothers who were still at home slept in what was called the Boys' Room. This was gloomy and always smelt of sweat.

I ran away from the first three infant schools I was sent to. My objections, even at the early age of five, were aesthetic. At the first one two girls with long pig-tails sat in front of me and cried all the time. So I joined them in crying, and when I realized that the teacher was in another room having tea, I ran home. At the second school we were made to stand in a queue while the teacher, who prided herself of being an amateur artist, drew whatever we requested on our slates. The girl in front of me asked for a mantelpiece and this was drawn for her. I wanted one as well, but with my limited vocabulary asked for a house instead. So she drew a house for me with smoke curling out of a chimney. I burst out crying, smashed my slate in front of her, and ran home. The third school was held in a converted garage and I objected because my brother, Douglas, attended a proper school called Trafalgar Junior. This time I refused to go after the first day. I remained at the fourth school because I fell in love with my teacher who was over-powdered, hairy and smelt heavily of perfume.

Although the White World seldom put in an appearance in District Six, we occasionally ventured out. These sorties were often hazardous and fraught with danger.

> I remember how my ragamuffin friends and I, bewitched by the lights and music of a Whites-only amusement park at the bottom of Adderley Street, cautiously advanced into it only to be chased out by a red-faced policeman.

> I remember the vice-squad raiding all the houses on Caledon Street for illicit liquor, and the huge, ugly detective in charge who poked through our wardrobe with a skewer.

> I remember the man who was later considered as one of Cape Town's most progressive mayors and a friend of the Blacks phoning the police to whip us off Green Point Track because we dare to practise our athletics there.

And the flaming torches carried by determined-looking Black men past Castle Bridge, protesting against segregation laws.

And my eldest brother, Joey, marching off to war in the Cape Coloured Corps in order to free Ethiopia from the ranks of his segregated unit.

And the first job I ever applied for. When I was asked to come for an interview, an embarrassed employment officer drew me aside and apologized because it was for Whites only.

And the unemployment queue in Barrack Street. After shuffling to the front I was told that with a Senior Certificate I was far too well qualified for any work they might offer.

And the White manager of a clothing factory who roared with laughter when I meekly indicated that I was looking for a position as a clerk.

You learn very soon that in the slums there is no real ethic other than one of accepting or rejecting. You either accept Jim Crow or you reject it. It is an ethic of survival. You soon learn how to feint, how to dodge, how to mask your resentment, how to insulate yourself against hurt by laughing too loudly or too wildly. You learn that the difference between colour discrimination and any other form is that colour is observable. And at the same time you blend into and try and seek anonymity with the mass. You become one with the other Blacks surrounding you for the purpose of Whites. But amongst yourselves you are not invisible, you are not fused with others, because the slum also teaches you early to guard your individuality jealously. When Whites are around you lose it purely as a protective device. But amongst yourselves you stake your claim to be different because you *are* different. Beneath your black skin beats a different heart. Beneath your wooly head beats a different thought. And your anti-Jim Crow ethic starts with the first dangerous thoughts and questions about that harsh, cold, White world outside. And you approach it not as a subservient but as an equal bent on answers. And this period is the most dangerous, not only because of the questions, but because of the answers. You adopt the ethics of an anti-Jim Crow.

Much of what I wanted to know I later found out in the books written by people who were able to articulate their experiences better than ever I could. From my Primary School days I read avidly and indiscriminately. By the time I was in High School my reading was in order to escape from the realities of the deprivation I saw surrounding me. I read furiously anything I could find, comics, detective stories, schoolboy yarns, romances. I never questioned the fact that all the good characters were White and that all the situations were White. I recall at the age of seven reading an elementary series about twins from different lands; the Eskimo twins and the Japanese twins and the Swedish twins. And when I came to the Nigerian twins the illustrations shocked and disappointed me because I had not catered for the fact that they were black. Surely all characters in books were White. Books were not written about people like me. Books were about a White Deerslayer who was condescending towards a Red Indian Chingakook. They were about a White

Huckleberry Finn who was condescending towards a Nigger Jim. So enormous was my appetite that I locked myself in the Boys' Room and tried to unravel the knotted language of *Measure for Measure* and Wordsworth's "Ode on Intimations." I scoured secondhand book stalls on the Grand Parade and spent my miserable allowance on volumes I hoped were classics and therefore respectable literature. I bought *The Complete Works of Sir Walter Scott* which was always on sale, and Milton's *Lycidas* and part two of *War and Peace* which was also always on sale. I quoted Shakespeare and Tennyson. I joined the run-down library at the Hyman Liberman Institute in Selkirk Street and took out *The Three Musketeers* and Rider Haggard's *She*, and a book whose title escapes me now but was about a nasty villain who sold innocent, unblemished White women to sex-crazed Cape Malays in the back streets of District Six. And in my innocence I was so impressed with content that I never bothered about purpose and intention.

But gradually, as I learnt to analyze my own position, I realized that the Scarlet Pimpernel was not on my side when he rescued rich aristocrats, that Tarzan was not on my side when he subdued Black tribesmen, that Kimball O'Hara was not on my side when he spied on Indian patriots. That because the literature I read was thematically White, I was denied an empathy with it as effectively as if it were done by official decree.

Then I read Richard Wright, Langston Hughes and Countee Cullen, and discovered Bigger Thomas and Cora, who was unashamed, and Big Boy, who left home, and Simple. I read *Uncle Tom's Children* and *The Ways of White Folks* and *Native Son* and *Cane* and *The Big Sea*. Peter Abrahams described the Johannesburg location in *Mine Boy* and described his life and mine in *Tell Freedom*. A new world with which I could identify opened up to me. I now knew that there were others who felt the way I did and, what was more, articulated it in a way I had never realized possible. I was now able to analyze my own situation through theirs, rationalize my own feelings through theirs. I could break with my literary dependence on descriptions by White folks and the Ways of White Folks. Native Son had come of age.

By the time I wrote my Senior Certificate examination my family position had improved to the extent that we had taken our first determined steps in to the ranks of the Coloured Middle Class. We moved from District Six to Walmer Estate. We spoke English at home instead of Afrikaans. However, I was not satisfied and somewhat skeptical about our improved social and economic position without a concomitant awareness. I started writing my first angry prose which was published by left-wing magazines and those catering for a Black readership since they were the only outlets prepared to publish the type of creative fiction we were producing. This brought me into personal contact with many other people, especially writers.

I am going to speak about two writers with whom I started close associations about that time. James Matthews is still alive but Ingrid Jonker is dead. Both suffered as writers because they were incapable of dealing with anything other than the truth.

By the time I was in my early twenties I had become friendly with an aggressive young journalist from Johannesburg who had just beem promoted to the local editorship of a tabloid newspaper geared at a Black readership. Moodley had been jailed during the Defiance Campaign, had been banned, and was a radical of sorts with a disarming smile and a puckish sense of humour. He had asked me to do a feature article entitled "My Sister was a Playwhite by Mary X." I was to be "Mary X." When I had finished I took it to his office at Castle Bridge and sat down at his desk to discuss it with him. The phone rang and while he was on the line a small, aggressive, unshaven young man of about my age, looking ostentatiously working class, shuffled in, nodded vaguely at Moodley, ignored me completely, and sat down in an opposite chair sinking his face into a magazine. For a brief moment Moodley stopped his telephone conversation, clapped his hand over the receiver, and said "Richard Rive — James Matthews."

So this was James Matthews whose stories I had recently read in the *Weekend Argus*, the telephone-operator who also wrote fiction in his spare time. He came from a slum area above Waterkant Street, even more beaten-up than District Six, had the merest rudiments of a secondary education and was reputed to be a member of a powerful gang. I think he saw in me everything he both envied and despised. I not only looked Coloured Middle Class, but I spoke Coloured Middle Class and behaved Coloured Middle Class. In spite of this initial setback to our relationship we overcame mutual suspicion and our friendship gradually cemented.

Quite some time after this unfortunate first meeting, by which time we were very close friends, I taxed him with hiding his home circumstances from me. I knew vaguely where he lived and that he was married with two small sons. "You really want to know where I live?" He arched his eyebrow threateningly. "Alright. Come home with me on Friday evening after office." He had by now succeeded Moodley on the newspaper.

I turned up determined not to be shocked at anything since I was sure that that was his purpose. We walked deep into the rough area above Bree Street, past mean gangs of thugs on mean corners. Near Pepper Street he paused in front of a door scarred with knife marks. We entered and stumbled up two flights of a gloomy staircase at the top of which we entered a surprisingly pleasant, sunlit room. The walls were lined with shelves filled with books. This was where James wrote. I sat down on a couch determined to be as sociable as possible. After a time I insisted on meeting his wife. He shouted at her down the staircase and a fresh-faced, attractive woman poked her head out and smiled shyly at me. He was on the point of dismissing her when I rose, introduced myself and shook hands. He smiled distantly.

James then insisted on our going to his local cinema, the West End in Bree Street. We sidled in through a back entrance and a door-keeper, who treated him with deference, allowed us in. The cinema was jammed with people who were sharing seats and sitting on the floor in the aisles. A dense pall of cigarette and dagga smoke hung low over the auditorium. In spite of the crowd one row of seats was completely empty. I realized then that no-one dared sit there as it was reserved for the gang of which James was an important member. We sat in the middle of this row with the luxury of unoccupied space around us. I was fully aware of the fact that had I not had the protection of James I would be in an extremely unpleasant situation. In fact I would never have been allowed through the entrance. I also realized that, in spite of a growing headache, I was the only member of the audience trying to concentrate on the movie. The rest were laughing, whooping, hurling around pleasantries and insults, gambling and selling illicit liquor and dagga. James sat, a man apart, indifferent to his surroundings, speaking earnestly to me about writing. I knew that he was out to teach me a lesson. I had wanted to go slumming and he was meting out the full treatment. What I do not think he realized was how familiar all this was to me, how I had sat in just such cinemas, the Star in Hanover Street, the British in Caledon Street and the National in William Street, watching *Zorro Rides Again* with crowds milling around in the auditorium. It was all so recognizable and all so painful.

Last year James came to my flat and thrust an official envelope at me. It stated tersely that his latest book of poetry which he had written in solitary confinement while in Victor Verster Prison, had been banned. He left me and went to his office to pack away all the copies of his collection with its zany title, *Pass Me a Meatball, Jones*. He left me to pack away a portion of his past. The bulldozers had moved in again.

Shortly after I had first met James in Moodley's office I qualified as a teacher and left our Walmer Estate home to board in Grassy Park and be nearer my school. I found lodgings with an aggressively respectable family which insisted on ignoring our shabbier neighbours and insisted on speaking English of sorts. By this time I was well acquainted with most of the writers in Cape Town and often visited Jan Rabie, the novelist, and his wife Margery Wallace, the painter, in Green Point. One evening Jan turned up at my place in Grassy Park with a few friends. Among them was a beautiful, withdrawn young woman with a wide-eyed, penetrating stare. She had already published a first book of poetry in Afrikaans and spoke intensely about it. This was Ingrid Jonker. We sat on the lawn of the house drinking wine and arguing, much to the horror of my landlord who was an elder in the local Dutch Reformed Mission Church. I was fascinated by Ingrid's intensity. I referred to her inadvertently as a poetess and she took me severely to task. She was a poet, no more, no less.

Our friendship progressed and became a very close one. We would sometimes ride around Cape Town on my scooter and pretend to be brother and sister because Margery Wallace said we looked alike and she felt motherly towards us. One evening we sat on the floor of Jan's house discussing South African politics. She drank in hungrily everything I had to say, then, after a long pause, turned her large, brown eyes on me and stated naïvely, ''I am so afraid that they will cut my throat.'' Suddenly the whole South African situation, all its discrimination, contradictions and injustices were focussed in her one fear. I never asked her what she meant, who would cut her throat. Would it be the Blacks thirsting for revenge, or the Whites furious at her unconventional standpoint? Metaphorically every innocent throat in South Africa is cut by bigotry and cant, and poets as well as non-poets are the victims.

We saw quite a bit of each other. Sometimes I would visit her; sometimes she would visit me; often we would meet at the same parties. She was always strange, sometimes withdrawn, sometimes impulsive, always unpredictable. At times she seemed like a spoilt child, at other times she seemed obsessed especially when discussing her poetry. Often she would laugh broadly when she tried to imitate an educated English accent.

After winning a major literary award she went overseas on her first trip outside South Africa. I was one of the very few people to see her off on the Union Castle liner Table Bay. She looked pleasant and trim in a petit costume. Then began her strange journey into the outside world. David Lytton, author of *The Goddam White Man* described some of this in an article called "Ingrid Jonker Comes to Stratford." I understood and appreciated what he described: the almost psychic web which she was able to spin around herself. Ingrid Jonker was like that.

And then on a brilliant morning in July, 1965, I was writing at my desk in Claremont near Cape Town, and the sunlight filtered through the open window, and a small transistor radio played softly in the background. The music stopped and an announcer said that the Afrikaans poet, Ingrid Jonker, had been found drowned at Green Point. She had taken her own life. And suddenly the morning turned grey for me. I rang Margery Wallace. She has tremendous self-control but this time she burst out crying and could hardly speak. But Ingrid had already died well before the waters of Green Point had lapped over her. As Nat Nakasa had already died well before he threw himself down a New York skyscraper during that same week. In a poem she called "I Want to Receive No More Visitors," Ingrid had spoken out strongly against her fellow White South Africans:

...the people living at the sea as though in the Sahara
the traitors of life with the face of death and of God.

We were a small, sullen group of writers at her funeral. Jan was there trying to organize. Jack Cope was beside himself and sobbing all the time. We stood desperately watching the ritual. James Matthews was next to me staring at the ground. And I remembered how when she gave me a copy of her first book *Ontvlugting* she had written in it, "Vir Richard — sonder die liefde is die lewe nutteloos." Without love life is worthless. And that same week Nat Nakasa died, and a few years later Arthur Nortje was also found dead in an Oxford room.

What better way to close this address than to bring together all we feel about South Africa, but especially about all the peoples who make up that sad land at the Southern edge of Africa. What better way to feel its temporary loss than to read the last verse of Arthur Nortje's poem, "Waiting" in which he shows all his nostalgia and yearning for the land he was never to see again.

You yourself have vacated the violent arena
for a northern life of semi-snow
under the Distant Early Warning System:
I suffer the radiation burns of silence.
it is not cosmic immensity or catastrophe
that terrifies me:
it is solitude that mutilates,
the night bulb that reveals ash on my sleeve.[3]

---

[3] Arthur Nortje, "Waiting," in *Dead Roots: Poems* (London: Heinemann Educational Books, 1973), pp. 90-91.

OUT OF THE GARDEN: NADINE GORDIMER'S NOVELS

John Cooke
University of New Orleans

Nadine Gordimer aptly observed in 1972 that "I have a strong sense of place," for her work is founded on the cultural references embedded in the South African landscape.[1] Her preoccupation with the landscape was clearly evident as early as 1954 in the title of an autobiographical fragment — "A South African Childhood: Allusions in a Landscape." Over the course of her career, these allusions gain depth. In the fifties, Gordimer functioned as a topographer of the bleak Witwatersrand and its garish metropolis of Johannesburg, until then almost uncharted in South African fiction. By the mid-sixties, she not only detailed the surface of this landscape but probed for its structural basis. In the terms she has employed, her focus shifted from "the surface shimmer" cast by her society to "what went on below ground...from where what matters most in human affairs often never comes up to light."[2] By the seventies, she used the landscape not simply to describe "what matters most," but to prophesy the African future reflected there. Over the years, then, Gordimer's role as an artist changes from that of topographer to prospector, from surveyor to seer of a new African cultural order.

This transformation of intention carried with it a change in technique, best approached through Gordimer's comments in "The Novelist and the Nation in South Africa" (1961):

> In South Africa, in Africa generally, the reader knows perilously little about himself or his feelings. We have a great deal to learn about ourselves, and the novelist, along with the poet, playwright, composer and painter must teach us. We look to them to give us the background of self-knowledge that we may be able to take for granted. Consequently the novel-in-depth — what one might call the "pure novel of the imagination — cannot be expected to flourish in Africa yet. We are still at the stage of trying to read ourselves by outward signs.[3]

Gordimer's semi-autobiographical *The Lying Days* (1953) is the personal attempt of a young English-speaking South African to find "a background of self-knowledge" in the "outward signs" of the landscapes she confronts. By 1963, in *Occasion for Loving*, Gordimer's protagonist perceives meanings in the landscape what are at once more socially inclusive and historically based. With *The Conservationist* (1975), the landscape becomes internalized, as reflected in the mind of the representative white South Africa Mehring. The meaning with which his imagination endows the land is Gordimer's vehicle for prophesying the

---

[1] "Writing in Africa: Nadine Gordimer Interviewed" (by Stephen Gray), *New Nation*, September, 1972, p. 2.

[2] "The Witwatersrand: A Time of Tailings," *Optima*, XVIII, 1 (January 1968), 22.

[3] *TLS*, 11 August 1961, p. 521; reprinted in *African Writers on African Writing* (Evanston: Northwestern University Press, 1973), pp. 35-36.

death of his kind and the reclaiming of the land by the Africans. With this novel, then, Gordimer provides the " 'pure' novel of the imagination," which she had felt beyond her scope, beyond that of South African novelists in general, a dozen years before.

Three of Gordimer's landscapes recur with such frequency that they warrant generic titles: "the garden," "the sea," and "the mine." The first is the term she uses repeatedly to describe the Edenic enclave from which her protagonists emerge to be educated in the realities of the South African world. "The gates of the garden are closing," she wrote in 1954, describing the urbanization which would make racial isolation even more difficult. "The push of something irresistible and cruel as the push of birth is carrying the people of Africa toward Johannesburg.[4] The experience of this cruel birth, the expulsion from the womb — like garden — one might say *laager* — is the instigating force in Gordimer's works. Indeed, the movement outside the white enclave is so arduous that it requires a series of births. Gordimer has described her early life as "my clumsy battle to chip my way out of shell after shell of ready-made concept," and Lionel Abrahams reports her more comprehensive application of the similar metaphor that "Someone growing up in a country like this had a whole series of cocoons to break out of."[5] What is finally required for Gordimer's protagonists to emerge from these shells, these cocoons, is a radical redifinition of the self in both personal and political terms. Gordimer persistently approaches this process through the subject of interracial sex. The central taboo of South African society and a political offense encoded in a byzantine structure of "Immorality Acts," sex across the color bar is the touchstone against which the personal development and political commitment of her protagonists is measured.

Gordimer employs the other two landscapes, the sea and the mine, in presenting the emergence from the garden to confront this taboo. The sea is associated with reflection, as a place where, distanced from the turmoil of the South African world, this threatening issue can manifest itself. It is the locale in which, to paraphrase Steyn in *Lord Jim*, one can "in the destructive element immerse." The protagonist of *Occasion for Loving* (1963), for exampes, comes to grips with interracial sex by the sea, where she "was no longer contained by walls but had a being without barriers," a state at once liberating and, since unregulated by the codes of a lifetime, disturbing.[6]

The mine functions in Gordimer's fiction as an image of the underlying basis of the South African world. What lies deep in the mine shaft is the desire which led whites to create the taboo. In 1968 Gordimer made these associations explicit when she used the mines as a metaphor for the psychic repression required in South African society:

The social pattern was, literally and figuratively, on the surface; the

---

[4] "Johannesburg," *Holiday*, 18 (August 1955), p. 50.

[5] "Leaving School-II: Nadine Gordimer," *London Magazine*, III, 2 (May 1963), 64. Abrahams' account is in "Nadine Gordimer: The Transparent Ego," *English Studies in Africa*, III, 2 (September 1960), 150.

[6] *Occasion for Loving* (New York: Viking, 1963), p. 196 Subsequent references in the text are to this edition.

human imperative, like the economic one, came from what went on below ground. Perhaps it always remained "below ground"; in men's minds too. It belongs to the subconscious from where what matters most in human affairs often never comes up to light.[7]

While the mine serves as the domain of the repressed throughout Gordimer's work, it is most clearly so at the close of *The Conservationist* in Mehring's paranoid fantasy at the mine dumps of being apprehended for an offense against the Immorality Act. Here, what remains "below ground" in the mine fully "comes up to light."

The persistent use of these three generic settings indicates, on the one hand, the coherent focus of Gordimer's work throughout the first two decades of her career. Beginning with *The Lying Days*, in which emergence from the garden is the theme and "The Mine" and "The Sea" two of the three section headings, these locales have been central to her work. The most sophisticated employment of them in *Occasion for Loving* and *The Conservationist*, on the other hand, is testimony to her increasingly penetrating view of her society and the concomitant development of her artistry in presenting this maturing vision.

> Gordimer has described *The Lying Days* as essentially about an experience many white South Africans have shared. They are born twice; the second time when, through situations that differ with each individual, they emerge from the trappings of colour-consciousness that were as "natural" to them as the walls of home and school...[8]

The concrete image of walls is appropriate, for Helen Shaw's rebirth in the novel is most strikingly reflected in her movement through the physical barriers created by her society. This is particularly true in "The Mine," in which the isolation of the white *laager* is conveyed through the barriers presented by the landscape. Gordimer provides here a sense of a situation she has explicitly described in the "The Witwatersrand: A Time of Tailings":

> one could go from christening to old age pension within the shelter of the company plantation of blue gums that surrounded the property. One need never be aware of the threatening space of the veld without. Inside the magic circle of blue gums everything was decided for one, from annual leave to social status...[9]

Moving from this womb-like society, Helen experiences a series of partial liberations from the world of her childhood. She first rejects the colonial society of the mines with its "cocoon-like quality," and her experiences with members of other ethnic and racial groups lead her to become part of the bohemian fringe of university students.[10] She eventually rejects this group when she becomes aware

---

[7] "The Witwatersrand...," p. 22.

[8] "English-Language Literature and Politics in South Africa," paper given at the conference on . Literature in the Conditions of South Africa, University of York, April 4-7, 1975. Quoted from page 12 of the lecture text. Ellipsis in the original.

[9] "The Witwatersrand...," p. 25.

[10] *The Lying Days* (New York: Simon and Schuster, 1953), p. 28. Subsequent references in the text are to this edition.

that for most of its members "it was only a stage in the process of becoming placid, conventional citizens," who would end up with "the elegant house apparently grown up round them as unavoidably as a tortoise grows its shell" (p. 142). After working in programs for urban Africans, she finally buckles under the heightened pressures of Nationalist-ruled South Africa and retreats first to a private world, which is like "being in a cage suspended from the invisible ceiling of the sky," and then, like the parents whose value she has tried to reject, to England, the standards of which had formed the basis of life within "the magic circle" (p. 259).

The cultural life of the whites within "the magic circle" consists of activities patterned on British models and in all matters exhibits "the identification of the unattainable distant with the beautiful, the substitution of 'overseas' for 'fairyland' " (p. 10). Helen, reared in this environment so at odds with that of the surrounding mine, finds it threatening to move outside it. The episode which opens the novel epitomizes the difficulty of her emergence. One Saturday, her parents reluctantly leave Helen alone, warning her not to leave the compound because "native boys" are about. She thinks this is "simply something to do with their mysteriousness" and decides to visit the Concessions outside:

> The mine houses had their fences and hedges around them, their spoor of last summer's creepers drawn up about their wall. I went down the dust road through the trees and out onto the main road that shook everything off from it, and that stood up alone and straight in the open sun and veld. It was different, being down on the road instead of up in the bus or the car seeing it underneath (p. 7).

When two "mine boys" pass, Helen has "a curious feeling" around her shoulders, but she continues to the Concessions, and feeling proud of her temerity on her return, she notices a mine boy standing apart:

> I had vaguely noticed them standing that curious way before, as I whisked past in the car. But as I passed this one I saw a little stream of water curving from him. Not shock but a sudden press of knowledge, hot and unwanted, came upon me. A question that had waited inside me but had never risen into words or thoughts because there were no words for it — no words with myself, my mother, with Olwen even. I began to run, very fast, along the tar, the smooth straight road...under the trees and up the road to the tennis courts (p. 13).

This episode sets the basic pattern for the novel. Helen ventures out from her parents' world, its isolation effectively presented here by the barriers of trees and fences and the contrast with the views from the car. The difficulty of transgressing the white norms is accentuated by posing the most threatening of consequences, the question without words, coming to terms with which serves as the touchstone against which Gordimer's protagonists are measured. Here, as metaphorically throughout the novel, "It was [the white enclave] to which the road brought me back always" (p. 18).

Helen seeks refuge repeatedly in other gardens throughout the novel. One instance occurs when she and a Jewish friend, Joel Aaron, drive to Mcdonald's Kloff, a rural area outside Johannesburg one afternoon. They sit on a rock and begin to trace an imaginary map of the world "rearranged to suit ourselves. We played with the discovering pleasure of children, ignored and watched by the Kloff and the sky'' (p. 128). Upon leaving the sheltered Kloff, however, Helen has an experience similar to her first trip outside the white compound. She steps on ''a rubber contraceptive, perished and dust-trodden, relic of some hurried encounter behind the trees, inconsequent and shabby testimony. But between us at that moment it was like a crude word, suddenly spoken aloud'' (pp. 128-129). While less overt than in the earlier scene, racial as well as sexual associations are here as well, for Joel has broached the subject of marriage, the idea of which Helen finds repellent due to the anti-Semitic views inculcated by her parents.

Helen finally fails to move outside the garden of her youth, and the reason for this failure is indicated by images associated with the sea. Her initial contact with the sea is pleasurable; the section of the novel headed ''The Sea'' details her initiation to sex by an older friend of the family. However, the sexual associations with the sea turn negative after she becomes established in Johannesburg. She begins, for instance, to view her sexual role as one in which ''I should lay myself down Ophelialike,'' and she and a lover make love ''unable to resist as the salmon is unable to deny his death leap upstream'' (pp. 199, 215). It is not until late in the novel that the sea becomes associated with threatening racial (and thereby political) thoughts as well. When, following the breakdown of a love affair, Helen seeks refuge within the white compound, for example, she looks outside the enclosure and begins to perceive ''rents and tears'' in it where ''the tops of the old fir trees which soughed about the Mine over the faint pant of the stamp batteries like the sea drowning the subterranean cries of its monsters'' (p. 281). The implicit association of ''the monsters'' with the African mining population is firmly established when Helen, having returned to Johannesburg, thinks of the impending general strike called by the African leaders:

> And over to the left, Johannesburg opened its mouth in its usual muffled roar. I could detect no note of panic — in any case, had there been screams, the howls of the monster at last risen staggering to its feet, they would have been blocked out for me by the indestructible brisk cheeriness of the radio next door (p. 291).

She does not escape the monster, however, for she and a friend are caught in a location during a riot precipitated by the strike. They first become aware of it when they hear an ''endless shout,'' ironically ''like the explosion of maniacal loudness that assaults you when you turn a radio volume full on by mistake'' (p. 299). Gordimer spares no pains to make the riot a seascape, the world that lurks beneath the surface of South African life. They see a mass of people as ''solid and writhing as a bark of fish in a net,'' the police attack is ''like a tidal wave churning through the crowd,'' a stone in the air is a ''watery zigzag,'' and after their escape they sit in a bar smiling at each other ''like people who have just been dragged up out of the water'' (pp. 291-301).

Gordimer has thus associated the sea with both sexual and political fears; it becomes the embodiment of all Helen needs to confront, and at the novel's close in Durban, it seems that she has indeed gone through a sea change. When Joel Aaron confesses that he had loved Helen even during her affairs with other men, she

> felt for a moment that my whole consciousness, resting since I was born on one side, had suddenly turned over, like a great stone on the bed of the

> sea, and shown an unknown world, a shining unseen surface, different,
> different utterly, alive with waving weeds and startled creatures pulsating
> on the coral (p. 337).

Helen has become aware of the sexual and political realities of this sea world, but
they finally prove too threatening. The novel ends with her seeking solace in the
world her parents had mimicked in the veld, as she expatriates, the sea providing a
passage to London. *The Lying Days* is, then, an account of the issues which must
be resolved if one is to emerge from the garden and the gates finally close, but the
commitments, sexual and political, needed to function outside prove too deman-
ding for Gordimer's first protagonist.

Occasion for Loving bears a strong resemblance to *The Lying Days*. At the
outset, Jessie Stillwell is within the sheltered white enclave; quite simply, "she
had never been out of the garden or challenged the flaming angels at the gates"
(p. 3). Unlike Helen, however, Jessie finally leaves the garden. Early on, she
correctly depicts her life as that of "a bird let into a series of cages, each one larger
than the last; and each one, because of its comparative freedom, seeming, for a
while to be without limit, without bars" (p. 17). *Occasion for Loving* shows her,
through vicarious involvement in a love affair between a black man and a white
woman, to have moved beyond the last of these cages. She, and perhaps her
husband, learn that outside the garden the sexual and political lives are inseparable, for "even between lovers they had seen blackness count, the personal return
inevitably to the societal, the private to the political" (p. 296).

Jessie's transformation is instigated by reflecting about the mines, the scene of
her upbringing. Through her reflections she becomes aware that South African
grows from an African history, not a European history as she had been educated to
believe; and she correlates this African history with her personal history, both of
which, she learns, have been denied through subterfuge. This connection of these
two buried histories is first introduced when she reflects on the difficulty of
retrieving her early experiences buried in her subconscious:

> There were signs that it was all still there; it lay in a smashed heap of
> rubble from which a fragment was often turned up. Her daily, definite life
> was built on the site of a series of ruined cities of whose history the
> current citizens know nothing (p. 21).

The metaphor, echoing Freud's use of the Eternal City to illustrate the simul-
taneous existence of all psychic experience in *Civilization and its Discontents*, is
particularly relevant to South Africa in the early sixties.[11] It was during this period
that ancient African kraals were discovered on the Witwatersrand, thereby shaking
the government's assertion that the division of land between races was based on
historical settlement. That Gordimer was particularly interested in the continuing
presence of past history is indicated by her comment in 1963 that "the *then* of
every country is contained in its *now*."[12]

---

[11] *Civilization and Its Discontents* (New York: Norton, 1962), pp. 16-18.

[12] "Party of One," *Holiday*, 34 (July 1963), p. 17. For discussion of the interest sparked by the
discovery of the remnants of the kraals, see John Lawrence, *The Seeds of Disaster* (London:
Gollancz, 1968), pp. 298-305. The uncovering of this information produced a change in Gordimer's
views; she had written in 1955: "That part of the Transvaal which later became the Witwatersrand
was not the settled home of any Bantu tribe" ("Johannesburg," p. 50).

It is during a visit to one of the weekly dances held on a mine near the one where Jessie grew up that the equation between the loss of the Africans' public past and Jessie's private past is made explicit. She watches the African miners dancing on the tarmac covering an Eternal City, the kraals of past times:

> unspeakable sadness came to Jessie, her body trembled with pain. They sang and they danced and trampled the past under their feet. Gone, and one must not wish it back. But gone...The crazed Lear of Africa rushed to and fro on the tarred arena, and the people clapped (p. 33).

Jessie cries tears which "came from horror and hollowness," and

> She held in her mind at once, for a moment, all that belonged to horror and hollowness, and that seemed to have foreshadowed it, flitting batlike through the last few days: the night in which she had awakened twice, once to her own sleeping house, and once to that time in her mother's house (p. 34).

The reason for Jessie's association of these two sets of events is clarified only later by the revelation that she had been denied her past by her forced seclusion from the normal adolescent activities due to both her mother's fabrication of a "heart disease," so as to remain the center of Jessie's affections, and deception about her true parentage. In short, the past presented to Jessie as her own is as bogus as the myths to the Africans of a Witwatersrand white from the beginning.

This equation of her personal history with the Africans' makes Jessie open to the destructiveness of more overtly related personal and political forces, namely the breakdown of the love affair between Gideon Shibalo and Ann Boaz due to the prohibitions of the Immorality Act. Jessie becomes aware of the developing affair earlier than others, but like Helen, she finds sex across the color bar initially too threatening a prospect to face and retreats to a private world on the Durban sea coast. This withdrawal proves impossible, for Ann and Gideon seek refuge with her. While initially resentful of their intrusion, Jessie finds a meaning in their arrival:

> This was not the Stillwell house where life was various. This place was completely inhabited for the present by *her being*; couldn't they sense it? — she thought: it must fill the place, like a smell. If they came here, it must be through some special and deeply personal connection with that being (p. 222).

By the end of their stay by the sea, Jessie has come to an awareness of the effect of "the question without words" on her life. As she finally tells Gideon,

> Do you know what I think while I look at you and Ann? Do you? I remember what was left out when I settled the race business once and for all. I remember the black men, who rubbed the floor round my feet, when I was twelve and fourteen...I used to feel, at night, when I turned my back on the dark passage and bent to wash my face in the bathroom, that someone was coming up behind me. Who was it, do you think? And how many more little girls are there for whom the very first man was a black man? The very first man, the man of the sex fantasies...Gideon, I'd forgotten. I'd left it all out. It's only when something like and Ann happens, one suddenly needs to feel one's way back (p. 267).

It is this awareness which leads Jessie to renounce her confortable Johannesburg existence. The extent of her change by the novel's close is indicated by her
more radical renunciation than her husband's of the liberal code that had informed
their lives:

> The Stillwell code of behavior was definitive, like their marriage; they
> could not change it. But they saw it was a failure, in danger of humbug.
> Tom began to think there would be more sense in blowing up a power
> station; but it would be Jessie who would help someone do it, perhaps, in
> time (p. 297).

Despite the qualifications in the final sentence, Jessie has quite clearly challenged
the angel at the garden's gates. She had noted during Gideon's first visit to their
home that he "had the slightly out-of-place look that she noticed Africans
sometimes had in a garden" (p. 118). *Occasion for Loving* is an account of her
learning to be out-of-place in it as well.

Superficially, *The Conservationist* bears little resemblance to *The Lying Days*
or *Occasion for Loving* because of Gordimer's radical departure from the traditional novel form. In contrast to the earlier novels, *The Conservationist* is com-
posed mainly of interior monologues which, as the novel progresses, come to
resemble "a jumping progression of bafflements in a tired man's mind."[13] The
novel is based, however, on the same landscapes as the preceding works: the
garden, the mines, and the sea (here transformed into a flood) carry the same
associations, but they exist not only objectively but as correlatives for develop-
ments in the psyche of Mehring, the novel's central figure. And *The Conservationist*, like the others, details a leaving of the garden. While the industrialist Mehring
marshalls all his energies toward remaining it it, the gates are forced upon by
suppressed impulses in him. Since Mehring does not gradually accommodate
himself to these impulses, his desires for sex across the color bar, he is unable to
deal with them as Jessie did and is finally overwhelmed when they suddenly erupt
from his subconscious.

The narrative is the account of Mehring's attempt to retreat from Johannesburg
to a small farm, his garden. His intention when purchasing the farm — to satisfy
"a hankering to make contact with the land" — is fulfilled, but in an unexpected
way.[14] Removed from the commercial world, Mehring finds his garden a place
where previously unacknowledged thoughts emerge. On the farm, Mehring can no
longer adhere to his maxim that "To keep anything the way you like it for yourself
you have to have the stomach to ignore — dead and hidden — whatever intrudes"
(p. 73). The body of a murdered African, found on the farm at the novel's outset,
serves to call up what lies "dead and hidden" in Mehring; through identification
with it, he becomes consumed with fears of death and renounces the farm.

The dead man beneath the land comes to represent what lies beneath the surface
of Mehring's mind. Lying one afternoon in the farm's field, Mehring begins to be
aware of "something already inhabited in imagination":

---

[13] This is Paul Theroux's description in "The Conservationist," *New York Times Book Review*, April
13, 1975, p. 4.

[14] *The Conservationist* (New York: Viking, 1975), p. 20. All subsequent references in the text are to
this edition.

I have my bit of veld and my cows...Perhaps he has dozed; he suddenly — out of blackness, blankness — is aware of breathing intimately into the earth. Wisps and shreds of grass of leaf stir there. It is the air from his nostrils that moves them. To his half-open eyes the hairs that border it and the filaments of dead grass are one.

There is sand on his lip.

For a moment he does not know where he is — or rather who he is; but this situation is which he finds himself, staring into the eye of the earth with earth at his mouth, is strongly familiar to him (p. 37).

Mehring has merged with the land, his hair blending with the "dead grass" and "earth at his mouth." He does not yet associate this experience with the dead African, which is, Mehring comes to think, "who he is."

This African is washed up following an apocalyptic flood, which is foreshadowed following Mehring's experience on this afternoon: "The sense of familiarity, of some kind of unwelcome knowledge of knowing, is slow to ebb. As it does, it leaves space in his mind or uncovers, like the retreat of a high tide, carrying away silt" (p. 37). This "unwelcome knowledge" is his repressed desire for an affair with a black woman, for when the African is washed to the surface — an image of the rising to consciousness of his "dark" and death-seeking thoughts — Mehring lapses into a fantasy of a sexual encounter with violent overtones at the Johannesburg mine dumps with a "coloured" girl.

The materials comprising Mehring's fantasy at the mine dumps derive from a trip he takes to Johannesburg late in the novel. Mehring picks up a hitchhiker, a young working-class woman, whom he will imagine is his partner during the fantasy. The associations with which their encounter is endowed are provided by Mehring's chance meeting in a coffee bar with the daughter of one of his business associates. Mehring makes a mild, avuncular advance, inviting her to a movie which the woman had mentioned in the car. Luckily for Mehring, the girl passes the suggestion off as a jest, for when he reads the morning paper, it is reported that her father had committed suicide in his car that very day.

This event intensifies Mehring's already powerful anxieties. He feverishly associates death and fears of exposures of his sexual desires with an array of the women in his life: his first woman as an adolescent, a Portugese girl on a plane trip, his mistress, the associate's daughter. "The excitation is suffocating; men have died in the act," he thinks, and his musings on the associate's death lead to the more practical thoughts of the best method for committing suicide. In doing so, Mehring provides a setting for his future encounter with the working-class girl:

Cyanide is the stuff that's used in the most effective and cheapest process for extracting gold from the auriferous reef. It is what saved the industry in the early 1900's. It is what makes yellow the waste that is piled up in giant sandcastles and crenellated geometrically-shaped hills where the road first leaves the city (p. 185).

The country's mining economy was built by the use of a material ideally suited for suicide; similarly, Mehring, one who has helped build this industry, is ruled by thanatos. At the mine dumps he is overpowered by a fantasy of sexual relations with a "coloured" girl which devolves into an imagined assault on himself.

When the dead African is uncovered by the flood, all that is "dead and hidden" surfaces for Mehring, the material dredged up from the mines representing his repressed sexual thoughts erupting into consciousness. The mine dump's texture, for example, reminds him of "the tiny snags of minute hairs when a forearm or backside cheek is brushed against lips," and the working-class woman is identified with this landscape: "The grain of skin is gigantic, muddy and course. A moon surface. Grey-brown layers of muck that don't cover the blemishes" (pp. 239, 246). As the fantasy spirals out of control, this woman becomes "coloured." "Oh God no," Mehring thinks, "That hair's been straightened and that sallowness isn't sunburn. That's it. Perhaps. It's a factory girl doing a grade of work reserved for coloured. A Sunday newspaper story" (p. 247). Mehring's defenses are finally strong enough for their imagined tryst not to be consummated; he imagines attackers, or perhaps the police waiting to arrest him, and he flees from the scene.

The the close of *The Conservationist* Mehring is in another country, and the novel ends with an account of his African laborers taking possession of his farm. For the first time in Gordimer's fiction, the white garden has ceased to exist. The flood, as in Genesis, heralds the death of one order, the birth of another. What remains at the close is not a garden, but simply the African land. On it, not Gideon Shibalo's people as in *Occasion for Loving* but Mehring's people seem out-of-place.

For Gordimer to end with this prophesy of the Africans reclaiming the land required perhaps the longest trek in the history of South African literature. Each of her successive works demonstrates more compellingly that the key to unlocking the garden's gates is identification with African culture. This theme is only implied in *The Lying Days*, in which Helen's absorption with British culture — life within "the magic circle" — keeps her from finally leaving the white garden. In *Occasion for Loving*, Jessie Stillwell does so by identifying with an African history, yet her full commitment lies in the future; she will throw the bomb "perhaps, in time." With *The Conservationist*, the future has arrived: the Africans have reclaimed their land, the buried kraals of which Jessie was fleetingly aware; and that even the conservative Mehring, who reviewers were quick to see as a representative white South African, has been compelled to submit to the sea's destructive element, to allow what lies in the mine shaft to "come up to light" implies that the opening of the garden's gates is inevitable for South African society.[15] *The Conservationist* marks the end of Gordimer's twenty-year treatment of this theme. For *Burger's Daughter* (1979), she takes as her epigraph a line from Lévi Strauss: "I am the place in which something has occurred." Gordimer's preoccupation with place remains, but the tense if, fittingly, now past, for her heroine Rosa Burger has lived outside the garden all her life.

Gordimer's prophetic vision called forth a change in her use of the novel form. *The Lying Days* and *Occasion for Loving* exhibit the dominant, and often stultifying, characteristics of post-war South African literature: in the first, the

---

[15] For comments on Mehring's representative nature, see Theroux, p. 4; and A.E. Voss, "The Conservationist," *Reality*, VII, 2 (May 1975), 16; and Christopher Hope, "Out of the Picture, *London Magazine*, XV, 1 (April/May 1975), 54.

documentary intention of providing a "background of self-knowledge" for her largely unexamined society; in the second, a sometimes too overtly political thrust, as in Jessie's thoughts on sabotage, growing from the increasingly truculent application of apartheid. In *The Conservationist* Gordimer subordinated these intentions to her prophetic vision of a South Africa manifesting its essentially African basis. Gordimer intimated the new form she would employ in setting forth this vision in a 1973 essay on Carson McCuller's essays. Gordimer wrote of McCuller that the key "aspect of her genius" was "carrying the societal ideas of her work in the living subconscious of her characters, transmuted into totally implicit actions and words." In *The Conservationist* Gordimer herself exhibits this genius. The documentary and political elements are "transmuted into totally implicit actions and words," and the core of the work is Mehring's subconscious, her vehicle for the expression of her "societal ideas." Through what might be termed Mehring's dying subconscious and the African reclamation of the land, Gordimer fashions what she had set as her goal in "The Novelist and the Nations in South Africa": a " 'pure' novel of the imagination." The place remains South Africa, but through the prophetic imagination of the novelist, the nation has clearly become African.

THE NORTH

A FEMINIST CRITIQUE OF THE ALGERIAN NOVEL OF FRENCH EXPRESSION

Mildred Mortimer
Haverford College

"Man is the outer lamp; woman is the inner lamp."[1] This Algerian Berber proverb succinctly acknowledges the two separate spheres of traditional North African society, male and female. Tradition dictates that the Muslim male function primarily in the public domain and the female remain almost exclusively within the confines of the home. Much ink has been spilled by sociologists, anthropologists, and historians, to explain that the two spheres which are clearly separate and in no way equal. Patriarchy has dominated North African culture often in an insensitive, unjust and violent way. Whether traditional or modern, the North African woman is dependent upon the male members of her family for status. Shc, as an individual, has littlc or no control ovcr hcr lifc or social position.[2] Hence, we may rephrase the proverb: "Man, the outer lamp, has power: woman, the inner lamp, has none."

In her study of women in the Mediterranean world, *Le Harem et les cousins*,[3] the French sociologist Germain Tillion concludes that the source of the problem of the subjugation of both North African Muslim and Southern European Catholic women lies in the Mediterranean concept of the ideal marriage. The perfect union is endogamous (i.e. between the children of two brothers), and the bride is a virgin. The the marriage remains with the family, a young bride moves from her father's protection to that of an uncle who assumes a parental role. This tradition is a poor guarantee of the bride's rights and proves to be none at all when the girl does not marry a first cousin. Moreover, the ideal of the bride's virginity places responsibility squarely upon the shoulders of her brothers. They are taught at an early age to be the guardians of their sister's virtue. Were a girl to lose her virginity before marriage she would not only disgrace herself but the family as well. Under the guise of protector, the brother may become a tormentor, for society encourages him to exercise power over women. He is expected to rule his sisters first, and then his wife and children, all the while encouraged and aided by his mother, a woman whose status was significantly improved by his birth.

Turning to the contemporary Algerian novel as it emerged in the post World War II period, we find the traditional concept of marriage under attack by both men and women writers. Evelyne Accad, in her study of North African Literature, *Veil of Shame*,[4] stresses the theme of sexual repression. Drawing primarily upon

[1] Basagana, Ramon et Ali Sayad, *Habitat traditionnel et structures familiales en Kabylie* (Alger: CRAPE, 1974), p. 43.

[2] Davis, Susan Schaefer, "Working Women in a Moroccan Village" in *Women in the Muslim World*, edited by Lois Beck and Nikki Keddie (Cambridge: Harvard University Press, 1978), pp. 417-433.

[3] Tillion, Germaine, *Le Harem et les cousins* (Paris: Seuil, 1966).

[4] Accad, Evelyne, *Veil of Shame* (Sherbrooke: Naaman, 1978).

the novels written by North Africans in the 1950's, Accad concludes that the fiction mirrors the reality, and that sexual repression in Maghrebian culture leads to tragedy for both men and women, but particularly for women. Accad notes the ways in which the theme is presented: adulterous love, women abandoned because of the exile or death of a partner, polygamy, repudiation, prostitution, female dishonor punished by death and vengeance.

No work contains all these themes. However, there is a consistent thread that runs through the literature. Woman is victim of her society. In studying the early novels of the 1950's, the works of Mohammed Dib, Mouloud Feraoun, Mouloud Mammeri, Marguérite Taos-Amrouche, Djamila Débèche, Assia Djebar, the reader finds that both the men and women writers share the same point of view. They depict the Maghrebian women, be she wife, mother, sister, or daughter, as a person locked into a repressive pattern. She is usually married off by her family in an economic transaction, then worn down through poverty and successive pregnancies, and is systematically prohibited from expressing herself. In a collection of sketches of Kabyle women, Feraoun bitterly condemns the abuse. He states:

> And Fatma n'Ahmed, do you remember her? Her story is banal too. Her parents doted on her because she was beautiful. The joy of life bloomed within her, the young men would wait for her on the path whenever she returned from the foutnain or from the field. But to her father, she was a luxury item to be given to the highest bidder. They married her off to the puniest of her suitors, the son of a family ridden with tuberculosis; he gave her his tuberculosis which he wore openly on his illness scarred face and a case of syphillis which nobody suspected. At the end of a year's time, Fatma was a horrible ghost, a body all bones and sores. She didn't take long to die, followed shortly thereafter by her sad husband. I cannot say it more emphatically. She was born to live and to love. She was born to run away with a young man as vigorous as herself, with others, with all of them. She was born to dishonor her family, to snub her nose at her father; she loved to sing, to dance, to dream. She should have died in a spasm of ecstasy, killed by an avenging bullet, the idiotic bullet that avenges implacable Kabyle honor. Yet she died of tuberculosis and syphillis, and instead of all the beautiful dreams of her stormy imagination, she only came to know a hideous nightmare. Her story deserves thought. Don't you think so, Amirouche?[5]

Writers such as Feraoun, critical of many aspects of Kabyle society, also express the conflict of the person who, having been born into traditional society and having had access to the Western world, finds himself caught between the two. Since many of the early works are largely autobiographical, male writers tend to choose young men as their protagonists and female writers, young women. Feraoun's angry young man, Amer n'Amer (*Les Chemins qui montent*) and Mammeri's rebel son Arezki (*Le Sommeil du juste*) have their female counterparts: Marie-Corail, the heroine of Taos-Amrouche's *Rue des Tambourins*, and Dalila, the rebellious young woman in Djebar's *Les Impatients*.

The four novels mentioned all record a young person's emotional development,

[5] Feraoun, Mouloud, "Destins de Femmes," *Algeria*, no. 44, nov-déc 1955, p. 10.

beginning first with the influence of the family. This is the sphere of the inner lamp, the hearth where the mother is prominent as conveyer of security, love, tradition. The focus changes in adolescence. External forces such as the colonial educational system, and outsiders, particularly French school teachers, assume importance. For the young man who will eventually become a cultural hybrid, participating in both the traditional and the modern world, the process necessitates an *itinéraire de lucidité*.[6] This is both a physical and spiritual voyage in which the protagonist gains a view of another world, new skills for a different environment, and a sense of self-understanding.

For the maturing young woman protagonist, the itinerary is not the same. Since she is not supposed to prepare for a public role, a young woman meets great resistance when she moves in that direction by pursuing her studies. Dependent upon the male members of her family for status and economic security, she must turn to her father, brother, or husband for permission to take the steps that lead further into the modern world. If a young girl avoids a marriage arranged by her family, she may meet a future husband who is willing to grant her the liberty that she longs for and that society refuses to give. In the literature — the novels of Djebar, Débèche, and Taos-Amrouche — the suitors are not enlightened individuals. They, like fathers and brothers, are portrayed as domineering and self-centered souls. Marie-Corail (*Rue des Tambourins*) meets one man who refuses to accept her as an adult and another who will not acknowledge her family traditions. The failing of each is the same: the inability to accept a woman as a total human being.

Caught between the conflicting value systems of East and West, the young women protagonists are unsure of their position in a society which is in transformation. In this respect, they confront the problem of the Western educated North African man. They nevertheless face a dilemma which is theirs alone, the question of control. Within the structure of a traditional marriage, there is clearly male domination. Within a modern, more sophisticated framework, male domination exists, but in a subtle form. We may call it the Pygmalion-Galatea syndrome. Neither Marie-Corail's suitor nor Dalila's fiancé may have ever heard of the mythological king of Cyprus who fell in love with the statue he had carved and which Aphrodite brought to life as Galatea. Yet, both act as if they had. Thus, Marie-Corail's beloved writes to her: "Each part of your soul and your body bears my stamp and my breath gives you life" (p. 282). Similarly, Djebar's heroine, Dalila, is told by her finacé: "You are a very little girl whom I will someday turn into a woman." She comments: "His tone was so filled with hope that I felt myself becoming the formless clay that he would mold in the future" (p. 205).

If, in the male's terms, to love is to control, the heroine can only rebel and retain her sense of self through her ability to elude her determined would-be captor. This quality, elusiveness, is central to the personality of another protagonist, Kateb Yacine's Nedjma. She is a fugitive who clings to independence, a fleeting gazelle who eludes all her potential captors. Nedjma's lover Rachid states:

> I had never seen such a woman in Constantine, so elegant, so savage, with the incredible air of a gazelle; one would have said that the clinic was

[6] Mouloud Mammeri stresses the importance of this theme in his work.

a trap, and that she was either about to collapse on those slim legs made for the trail, or to suddenly escape, at the first gesture that anyone would dare make towards her. (*Nedjma*, p. 107).

Nedjma is a major novel of contemporary North African fiction. It is important to feminist criticism because it is the first work to present woman as a goddess. Throughout this novel and the subsequent work, *Le Polygone étoilé*, Nedjma — star, in Arabic — remains elusive and mysterious. She does not reveal herself, but her presence is felt through her effect upon the other characters. She appears as a dangerous temptress of obscure origine, *l'ogresse au sang obscur*, Her symbolic presence is heightened in the novel as the temptress and the lost nation, Algeria, become one. Then Nedjma's lover, Rachid, speaks of his homeland as "the land of the setting sun which saw born, sterile, marked by destiny, Nedjma, our ruin, the unlucky star of our clan" (p. 188).

They myth of Nedjma is transparent. She is Algeria, *la patrie perdue*. Pursued by four potential conquerors — Turk, Roman, Arab, French — she embodies the characteristic which the Algerian poet and critic Jean Amrouche first attributed to the Maghreb: *le génie de l'alternance*, the elusiveness of the captive. The conquerors are subtly transformed by their prisoners. When Nedjma speaks of her hypnotic power, she explains: "Since they love me, I keep them in my prison…In the long run, it is the prisoner who decides…" (p. 67). In Kateb's subsequent Novel, *Le Polygone étoilé*, published after Algerian independence, the mysterious cloistered Nedjma is transformed into a goddess of action: "Here she is as the height of her legend, after absurd persecutions, here she is in spite of the fact that she had been assumed dead; for we had lost her in the war, lost, reconquered, and nothing threatens her as much as the rage of her own warriors; we love her too much, and in love, we are ferocious" (p. 145).

Kateb emphasizes woman as goddess, but he also presents woman as victim. In his world, the lover is a goddess; the mother is a victim. Therefore, Nedjma's lover Mustapha keeps a diary in which he depicts his mother. She is a native woman garbed in her veil, forced by custom to silence and seclusion. Mustapha writes: "Her dream is to go out with my father, as the sound of his cane grows fainter" (p. 211).

As a child, Mustapha comes to know the glow of the inner lamp. He is very close to his mother and appreciates the environment she provides for him. Later, his father forces him to enter the French school system. At this point, he begins to move away from his mother. The bonds between them weaken.

The contrasting images of woman as goddess/woman as victim also appear in the work of the Algerian novelist and poet, Mohammed Dib. Whereas Kateb juxtaposes both images within the same work, Dib separates the two. Yet both novelists, alternating between realism and surrealism, reserve the former prose style for the victim and the latter for the goddess.

Dib's first novel, *La Grande Maison*, explores the relationship between mother and son and reveals its ambivalent nature. An impoverished, exhausted widow, Omar's mother often attacks her son verbally, sometimes physically. Yet, when the boy is frightened, she is there to comfort him. *Dar-Sbitar*, the big house, and A'ini, Omar's mother, are the boy's refuge against a brutal world. Because of his strong attachment to his mother, Omar leaves school when traditional values and French colonial teachings come into conflict.

Dib plays upon a homonym: *la mer, la mère*. Just as the Mediterranean sea separates Algeria from mainland France, A'ini, Omar's mother, provides the barrier between his world and that of this pseudo-compatriots, the French. Dib returns to this homonym in the symbolic novel, *Qui se souvient de la mer*. This work which expresses the horror of the Algerian war in surrealistic terms, presents the goddess Nafissa (soul). In a city which is calcifying, and therefore dying, the only hope for life remains with life giving forces, women and the sea. "Without the sea, without women, we would have remained definitively orphans" (p. 21). The protagonist Djamal is saved from death because his spouse, Nafissa, is able to lead him to an underground refuge. Unlike Kateb's Nedjma who is sterile and unfaithful to men, Dib's Nafissa is an exemplary wife and mother. Leading Djamal and their children to safety, Nafissa is a protector as well as a life giving force.

The theme of woman as goddess is significantly absent from the work of Algerian women writers. Nedjma and Nafissa are idealized expressions of a man's dream, not of a woman's. It is important to note that the theme does not reappear in the work of younger Algerian male writers. For example, Rachid Boudjedra, younger than Kateb and Dib, as innovative and lyrical, rejects the image of woman as goddess and gives new expression to the theme of woman as victim. Boudjedra's first novel, *La Répudiation*, which he states reflects the tragedy of his older sister's generation,[7] concerns the effect upon a family of the questionable form of Muslim divorce; a wife may be condemned by a patriarch's whim. There are several forms of repudiation, or rejection in the novel. The protagonist rejects the Algerian political structure which has allowed a technological bureaucracy to betray revolutionary ideals. He also rejects the traditional Algerian bourgeois society as represented by his corrupt father. Most important, he is traumatized by his father's repudiation of his mother. As a psychological drama, *La Répudiation* is reminiscent of the Moroccan novelist Driss Chraibi's work, *Le Passé simple*. Chraibi also presents a son who rebels against the autocratic father responsible for his mother's suffering.

In Boudjedra's world, suffering — both physical and psychological — is inflicted upon society's victims: women and young children. Blood, symbolic of sacrifice, is a constant motif in *La Répudiation* and the subsequent work, *L'Insolation*.

In a central portion of the first novel, Boudjedra describes the horror of children forced to watch the sacrificial slaughter of a lamb for a Muslim religious holiday. For the children, this bloodletting is linked to the fear that harm may come to their mothers who, through menstruation, also bleed. Blood, representing woman's physical suffering, is emphasized once more when the patriarch, having repudiated his first wife, marries a fifteen year old girl. The proof of the young girl's virginity is the abundance of blood on the sheets.

In the subsequent novel, *L'Insolation*, Boudjedra transforms the theme of

---

[7] Lecture by Rachid Boudjedra on May 18, 1978 at the Faculté des Lettres, Université d'Aix en Provence, France.

defloration. When the protagonist makes love to a young student, she rejoices in losing her virginity. Breaking with tradition, Samia is liberated. Boudjedra, like the novelists who precede him, calls for a break with tradition. The legacy of the endogamous marriage is the inqueality of experience and accompanying lack of communication and understanding between spouses.

Algerian male writers, from Feraoun to Boudjedra, have treated the subject of inequality between the sexes with compassion and have called for an end to patriarchal oppression. Thus, both men and women writers in Algeria express the same concern, but grapple with it from different positions. The women writers see themselves in the victim; the men writers view the victim as someone else.

A very sensitive portrait of women appears in Assia Djebar's novels, *Les Enfants du nouveau monde* and *Les Alouettes naives*, both published after the Algerian war. In these works, Djebar presents the psychological and sociological complexities of women's position in contemporary Algeria. She examines the problems confronting women who are trying to liberate themselves from an oppressive cultural pattern. The first novel presents a group of women of varied life styles all challenged by the fact of war during the Algerian revolution. These women assume their individual responsibility within the collective struggle for independence. Each one moves from the position of passive bystander to that of active participant.

Les Enfants du nouveau monde is the affirmation of woman as an individual. *Les Alouettes naives* changes the focus to woman as a marriage partner. In the latter novel, Djebar creates a more personal world. Probing the complexities of a marriage, she explores the relationship as emotional and sexual fulfillment for both partners.

With its flashbacks, rapid changes of scene, disregard for chronology, focus on childhood memories, *Les Alouettes naives* is reminiscent of Kateb Yacine's *Nedjma*. However, the goddess is absent. Moreover, the past as evoked by Djebar's heroine, Nfissa, is free from the anguish expressed by Kateb's protagonists. More important to Djebar's novel than the past is *au-dela* — time beyond — the period of time that the couple Rachid and Nfissa, share with each other in an atemporal paradise.

The sense of awakening and responding to one another physically and psychologically moves them beyond life's daily routine and transports them to a temporary Eden. There, they live intensely and, for a brief time, exist only for each other. However, this intensity cannot be sustained. External demands, specifically the pressure of war, force them apart. When Rachid leaves for *maquis*, the war zone, Nfissa does not follow him. Once married, she stays behind and withdraws significantly from political activity. Questioned about her herioine's retreat, Djebar explains: "Perhaps I am not very modern. But it seems difficult for a woman to succeed fully in both her personal life and in her social commitment.[8] This statement tells us that neither the writer nor her protagonist can truly integrate the two spheres, the worlds of the inner and the outer lamp.

Djebar's couple does make important gains. Rachid and Nfissa require and

---

[8] Hennebelle, Monique, "La Femme sera le devenir du monde arabe: Une interview d'Assia Djebar," *L'Afrique littéraire et artistique*, no. 3, février 1969, p. 62.

recognize maturity for themselves. They break with the traditional ideal of the endogamous marriage. *Les Alouettes naïves* ends upon a note of tempered optimism. The couple must learn to live together once again after the war has ended; they must re-establish communication and intimacy. Both partners realize that the task will not be an easy one.

Until greater social and political equality have been achieved in Algeria, women writers such as Assia Djebar will continue to use fiction as a weapon against injustice. Her work has inspired a younger generation. Thus, Aïcha Lemsine's novel, *La Chrysalide*, picks up and reworks the same themes and preoccupations of Djebars *Les Enfants du nouveau monde*, published fourteen years earlier. Both novels express the collective identity of Algerian women during a crisis. In addition, they both portray a modern and a traditional heroine. The purpose is the same: to show that women formed by a culture that insists upon submission can indeed free themselves from society's shackles and participate actively in life. Given this goal, Djebar's heroines are more militant than Lemsine's. In Lemsine's novel, only one woman, the village nurse, actually participates in the war effort.

In *La Chrysalide*, the struggles and hardships of Khadidja, a traditional woman, dominate the first part of the work, and those of her stepdaughter Faíza, a young girl moving into the modern world, the second. A brilliant student, Faíza studies medicine and becomes a doctor. Yet, like all Maghrebian women, she depends upon a male member of her family for support, both economic and psychological. When Faíza's brother allows her to continue her studies, the writer explains: "Mouloud was the Pygmalion of Faíza' spirit" (p. 170). Faíza and her brother, Mouloud, adhere to the traditional precept: a brother is responsible for his sister. Once again, a variation of the Pygmalion-Galatea syndrome reappears.

Like Djebar's Nfissa, Faíza cannot integrate the two spheres: the inner and the outer worlds. Whereas Djebar's heroine achieves emotional fulfillment but withdraws from public commitment, Faíza succeeds in her professional role but loses her chance at love and marriage. The young woman doctor who returns to her village to practice medicine is an unwed mother. Faíza will live with her stepmother, raise her child, and cherish fond memories of her fiancé who was killed before they could marry. Djebar's couple is separated temporarily by war; Lemsine's is doomed because of an automobile accident — the cruel hand of fate.

Why does Lemsine deny her heroine a life of happiness? There are two equally plausible and conflicting answers. Perhaps she is too conservative, or believes that her reading public is, to allow a young woman who has broken with the traditional attitudes towards virginity to achieve happiness. Or, perhaps Lemsine has discarded the dream of the perfect couple, finds greater strength in sisterhood, and prefers to end the novel on a note of female solidarity.

It is fitting that this study end with a question, for Algeria is a nation in transition with many unanswered questions, puzzles, and contradictions. The position of women in the society should remain one of its major concerns. Traditionally excluded from public places, the Algerian woman is present in modern literature. The quest for identity which has continually preoccupied North African writers is her quest. When she is no longer perceived either as victim or as goddess, then she will have truly arrived.

BIBLIOGRAPHY

ACCAD, Evelyne. *Veil of Shame*. Sherbrooke: Naaman, 1978.

BASAGANA, Ramon et Sayad, Ali. *Habitat Traditionnel et structures familiales en Kabylie*. Algiers: CRAPE, 1974.

BECK, Lois and Keddie, Nikki, eds. *Women in the Muslim World*. Cambridge: Harvard University Press, 1978.

BITTARI, Zoubeïda. *O, mes soeurs musulmanes, pleurez!* Paris: Gallimard, 1972.

BOUDJEDRA, Rachid. *La Répudiation*. Paris: Denoël, 1969.

_____ *L'Insolation*. Paris: Denoël, 1972.

CHRAIBI, Driss. *Le Passé simple*, Paris: Denoël, 1954.

Débêche, Djamila. *Aziza*. Algiers: Imbert, 1955.

DÉJEUX, Jean. *Littérature maghrébine de langue française*. Sherbrooke: Naaman, 1973.

DIB, Mohammed. *La Grande maison*. Paris: Seuil, 1952.

_____ *L'Incendie*. Paris: Seuil, 1954.

_____ *Le Métier à tisser*. Paris: Seuil, 1957.

_____ *Qui se souvient de la mer*. Paris: Seuil, 1962.

_____ *Cours sur la rive sauvage*. Paris: Seuil, 1964.

_____ *Dieu en Barbarie*. Paris: Seuil, 1970.

DJEBAR, Assia. *La Soif*. Paris: Julliard, 1957.

_____ *Les Impatients*. Paris: Julliard, 1958.

_____ *Les Enfants du nouveau monde*. Paris: Julliard, 1962.

_____ *Les Alouettes naïves*. Paris: Julliard, 1967.

_____ *La Terre et le sang*. Paris: Seuil, 1953.

FERAOUN, Mouloud. *Le Fils du pauvre*. Paris: Seuil, 1954.

_____ *Les Chemins qui montent*. Paris: Seuil, 1957.

_____ *L'Anniversaire*. Paris: Seuil, 1972.

KHATIBI, Abdelkabir. *Le Roman meghrébin*. Paris: Maspéro, 1970.

LEMSINE, Aîcha. *La Chrysalide*. Paris: Des Femmes, 1976.

MAMMERI, Mouloud. *La Colline oubliée*. Paris: Plon, 1952.

_____ *Le Sommeil du juste*. Paris: Plon, 1955.

_____ *L'Opium et le bâton*. Paris: Plon, 1965.

M'RABET, Fadéla. *La Femme algérienne*, suivi de *Les Algériennes*. Paris: Maspéro; 1969.

TAOS-AMROUCHE, Marguerite. *La Rue des Tambourins*. Paris: Table Ronde, 1960.

TILLION, Germain. *Le Harem et les cousins*. Paris: Seuil, 1966.

YACINE, Kateb. *Nedjma*. Paris: Seuil, 1956.

_____ *Le Polygone étoilé*, Paris: Seuil, 1966.

YÉTIV, Isaac. *Le Thème de l'aliénation dans le roman maghrébin d'expression française*. Sherbrooke: CELEF, 1972.

TAOS AMROUCHE, FABULISTE

Claude Chauvigné
Guilford College

"Les Berbères, dit Ibn Khaldoun au XVe siècle, racontent un si grand nombre d'histoires que, si on prenait la peine de les mettre par écrit, on en remplirait des volumes."[1]

Taos Amrouche est décédée le 2 avril 1976, à l'âge de 63 ans, et ses obsèques eurent lieu à Saint Michel de l'Observatoire. Elle était née le 4 mars 1913 á Tunis où sa famille avait émigré en quête de travail. Cette famille de souche kabyle algérienne devait laisser des marques sur la littérature française puisque la mère, Fadhma Amrouche écrivit un émouvant roman autobiographique, *Histoire de ma vie* (1968), et un de ses frères, Jean Amrouche, fut reconnu comme un authentique poète. La vie de la famille Amrouche fut très mouvementée: innombrables déménagements, difficultés matérielles et sociales, peines et maladies abondent. Pourtant, Taos put faire de bonnes études à l'Ecole Normale de Sèvres, séjourna quelque temps en Espagne, puis vint s'établir définitivement en France au lendemain de la Deuxiéme Guerre Mondiale, et prit part aux activités culturelles de la radiodiffusion française — récitals de chants et contes berbères, tournées et autres manifestations artistiques. En plus, nous devons noter qu'elle est l'auteur d'ouvrages quie reçurent nombreux éloges: *Jacinthe noire* (1947), *La Rue des tambourins* (1960), *L'Amant imaginaire* (1975), *Le Grain magique* (1976). Enfin à titre biographique mais aussi d'intérêt général, nous rappellerons qu'elle fut l'épouse du peintre André Bourdil et que leur fille, Laurence, fait une brillante carrière au théâtre.

Voici ce qu'écrivit Josanne Duranteau (voir «Hommage à Taos Amrouche» dans *Le Monde*, 4 avril 1976, p. 17) saluant la mémoire de cette belle figure: "Taos Amrouche qui vient de mourir, se savait atteint d'un mal incurable. Elle n'en avait pas moins la vaillance de chanter les magnifiques chants berbères que ses disques sauvent de l'oubli. Sa ferveur savante avait su recueillir à sa source la tradition la plus rare et la plus fragile d'une culture orale dont les rythmes étaient ceux de son propre coeur."

Ce sont ces rythmes, dans un très large entendement, que nous allons essayer ici de cerner et de présenter.

Pour mieux saisir la teneur de ce travail il convient de rappeler brièvement la nature du conte. Celui-ci, à la différence de la nouvelle et du roman, ne cherche pas à nous donner une impression de la réalité mais à nous dépayser par le merveilleux, la féerie, le fantistique et le mystère. Par ailleurs, il tend à styliser la réalité pour amuser ou pour instruire. C'est dans cette définition que se place l'oeuvre de Taos Amrouche *Le grain magique*. Trois aspects en seront ici présentés — les thèmes, les personnages et le style — et quelques extraits serviront à illustrer ce monde Kabyle (berbère) "dans son expression la plus authentique" et, au dela, "une poésie cosmique."[2]

---

[1] Taos Amrouche, *Le grain magique* (Maspéro, 1976) p. 9.   [2] Ibid, couverture.

Examinons donc pour commencer la nature des thèmes et leur traitement. Celui de la jalousie est certainement l'un des plus divers et des plus développés de ce recueil. La jalousie entre frères: l'aîné d'une famille "laid, sournois, morose et déplaisant" envie son jeune frère "beau, tendre et gracieux". Or la mère que veut faire de son aîné un homme le soigne avec attention, mais voulant le préparer aux rudesses de la vie le gâte moins que le cadet. Il s'ensuit inévitablement des dissensions entre les frères. "La jalousie germa dans le coeur de l'aîné et grandit comme une méchante plante épineuse et noire."[3] Le frère aîné finira par tuer son cadet en le poussant du haut d'un rocher.

La jalousie entre soeur et belle-soeur: un frère et sa soeur, Reskia, vivent heureux et paisibles dans leur maison. Ils sont unis, se comprennent, s'admirent mutuellement et sont entièrement dévoués l'un à l'autre. Cependant, la soeur désirant un bonheur complet pour son frère se met en quête de lui choisir une femme. Celle-ci ne peut longtemps supporter l'entente qui règne entre son mari et sa belle-soeur; elle devient jalouse.[4] La haine s'accumule dans son coeur et un jour elle fait manger des oeufs de serpent à Reska dont le ventre se gonfle et le teint se ternit. Poursuivant la jeune femme de sa haine implacable, elle l'accuse d'avoir déshonoré la famille et persuade son mari de la tuer.

La jalousie entre père et fils: le père envie le somptueux palais de son fils et les femmes éblouissantes de beauté dont celui-ci s'est entouré, et "la jalousie était en lui comme un feu dévorant."[5] Par trois fois, il essayera de lui arracher la vie en utilisant différents moyens plus cruels les uns que les autres (poison, fosse hérissée de glaives et de poignards, et chainette d'argent maléfique). Pourtant, le fils échappe à ces attentats et condamne (non sans quelques regrets) son père au bûcher.

La jalousie entre marâtre et enfants: la femme ne pouvant supporter les enfants du premier mariage poussera leur père à les supprimer ou à les abandonner.

La jalousie entre bru et belle-mère: la jeune épouse voulant être seule maîtresse de son foyer ne sera satisfaite que lorsqu'elle aura convaincu son mari de couper la tête de sa mère, lui arracher le foie et le lui apporter en gage d'amour.[6]

Toutes ces manifestations et ces actes nous paraissent extrêmes et barbares. En fait, il semble bien que c'est "combattre le feu par le feu" — par ces exemples. le narrateur — ici Taos Amrouche — veut prouver à son auditoire l'horreur de la jalousie. Somme toute: leçon de morale que l'on retrouve chez tous les fabulistes. Il nous vient précisément à l'esprit quelques-uns des merveilleux contes de Birago Diop, tel *les Mamelles*, histoire de deux femmes affligées inégalement d'infirmités. Celle-là, Khary, avait "une toute petite bosse de rien du tout;[7] celle-ci, Koumba, était bossue "mais sa bosse dépassait vraiment les mesures d'une

---

[3] Ibid. p. 79.

[4] Ibid. p. 192.

[5] Ibid. p. 192.

[6]Ibid. p. 6.

[7] Birago Diop, *Contes choisis*

honnête bosse.''[8] Or Khary acariâtre et méchante envie la douce et gaie Koumba dont la bosse disparaîtra par magie précipitant ainsi la crise de jalousie à son terme fatal.

Dans le cadre didactique et moralisateur de ces contes un autre thème revient sans cesse: la passion. Il ne s'agit pas seulement du sentiment que deux êtres peuvent éprouver l'un pour l'autre, mais de celui-ci poussé par quelque abérration dans une direction tout autre et très souvent néfaste.

C'est ainsi que se présente la passion d'un prince pour sa belle femme. Si la psychologie de cette passion n'est pas approfondie, par contre la beauté de la femme aimée est décrite avec grandes précisions: "elle était blanche et rose, lumineuse, et ses abondants cheveux la couvraient d'or jusqu'à la taille.''[9] Pour elle le prince accomplira des prouesses de plus en plus dangereuses. Mais tandis qu'il se plie aux caprices de sa femme, celle-ci s'ingénie par tous les moyens à le tromper avec un ogre diabolique. Le méchanceté et l'infidélité de ''la jeune femme au coeur noir'' seront finalement exposées, et après avoir tué l'ogre et vengé son honneur, le prince abandonnera sa perfide épouse.

Dans un autre récit par contre, l'amour profond de la femme est développé avec finesse. Cette femme est douce, chaleureuse, intelligente, et par bien des aspects, supérieure au prince, son mari. Celui-ci ne peut supporter naturellement cet état. Il s'en suivra séparation des époux; mais séparation provisoire puisque l'intelligente princesse, par son intuition, sa clairvoyance et son amour, regagnera l'affection de son mari.

Un autre thème encore que soustend l'action de nombreux contes concerne l'importance des liens familiaux; la loyauté et la cohésion de tous les membres unis par un même coeur. Ainsi *Les Chevaux* d'éclairs et de vent, qui incidemment ressemblent à la fable de La Fontaine *Les deux pigeons*. En effet, il s'agit de deux frères dont l'un veut découvrir le monde tandis que l'autre, moins curieux mais aussi plus sage, préfère rester à la maison où une vieille mère a besoin de sollicitude. Cependant ce conte diffère de celui de La Fontaine par une originalité toute particulière: l'introduction d'un élément féerique (les feuilles d'un arbre tout spécial qui jauniront si le frère aventureux se trouve en difficultés) joue un rôle important. Les feuilles de l'arbre magique jauniront un jour: "un malheur est arrivé à mon frère, je pars,''[10] et aussitôt le sédentaire de se précipiter au secours du frère voyageur qu'il ramène à la maison avec son épouse et son enfant. La description de ce retour éclate d'allégresse; "Les jumeaux sentaient déjà l'odeur de la terre natale. Ils allaient, ils allaient joyeux sur leurs chevaux d'éclairs et de vent et la princesse, sur sa jument bleue, partageait leur joie.''[11]

Notons aussi le thème de la gourmandise qui nous étonne au premier abord. Pourtant, quand nous songeons à la pauvreté de ces montagnards et à leur frugalité, nous pouvons bien les excuser d'excès qui chez d'autres peuples seraient

[8] op. cit.

[9] Taos Amrouche, *Le grain magique*, p. 117.

[10] op. cit. pp. 90.

[11] op. cit. p. 95.

sans doute de gros défauts sinon des péchés.

La gourmandise revient donc assez souvent dans les contes mais presque toujours poussée à un extrême qui est évidemment plus symbolique que réel. Précisément, voici ce conte *Ma Mère m'a égorgé, mon père m'a mangé, ma soeur a rassemblé mes os*[12] dans lequel la gourmandise est d'abord traitée selon la définition que nous lui attribuons normalement, toute proche de la gloutonnerie; puis par une aberration qui n'a plus rien d'humain, elle se transforme en une scène d'horreur. Il s'agit de cette femme qui ayant mangé toute la viande du couscous ne trouve rien de mieux que de la remplacer par son enfant coupé en petits morceaux. Evidemment, il ne faut voir dans cette barbarie qu'une expression subconsciente de privations intenses et endémiques. Mais aussi, et c'est peut-être là le message caché de ce conte, par la voix du narrateur c'est la terreur qu'inspire le mari et l'affreuse réalité de la condition feminine en pays musulman qui sont dévoilées. Dans l'un et l'autre cas, la démesure devient explicable et logique, abstraction faite de l'humain et en particulier de l'humain maternel.

Les thèmes des contes de Taos Amrouche sont donc bien porteurs de messages, de sujects à réflexions, d'introspections subtiles dans le mileiu et dans la mentalité de son peuple farouche et simple.

De même les personnages des contes concrétisent des idées centrales, essentielles, et donnent dimension aux histoires (et à l'enseignement) qui sont présentées. Ils sont nombreux ces personnages, parfois simplifiés ou grossis, et ils illustrent de façon didactique les aspects multiples et complexes de la nature humaine. Souvent, ils échappent aux lois de la vie ''normale.'' En effet, géants, nains, êtres bizarres entourés d'enchantements apparaissent, se métamorphosent, disparaissent et resurgissent magiquement devant nous. Ces personnages sont soit des caricatures de l'homme soit des créations poétiques qui évoquent nos rêves et nos désirs de perfection, ou qui crystallisent notre sensibilité grâce à l'introduction de fées, d'anges et de princesses.

Arrêtons-nous à quelques-un de ces personnages choisis tout particulièrement pour leur ubiquité car ils réapparaissent très souvent dans ce recueil, et pour leur personnalité bien affirmée.

Voici Settoute la vieille sorcière qui est méchante, hypocrite et rancunière. Elle porte en elle une ombre haineuse dont elle ne peut se délivrer tandis qu'elle révèle une redoutable puissance: elle jette des sorts sur les gens auxquels elle veut du mal et cela pour des raisons toutes personnelles; elle a à sa disposition des pouvoirs magiques et n'hésite nullement à s'en servir pour détruire ses ennemis.[13]

Voici Tsériel[14] l'ogresse et ses semblables: l'ogre et les ''sept ogres.'' Ce sont des géants qui symbolisent évidemment la force aveugle, brutale et dévoratrice. Ils sont obsédés de destructions et ont besoin de leur ration quotidienne de chair fraîche. Parfois, il est possible de les jouer, de les tromper (en leur faisant avaler leurs propres enfants par exemple), mais trop souvent leur perversité s'affirme supérieure et victorieuse. Sont-ils l'image du temps qui s'engendre et se dévore

---

[12] op. cit. pp. 107-110.

[13] op. cit. ''Le grain magique,'' pp. 13-18.

[14] op. cit. ''Loundje, fille de Tsériel,'' pp. 21-26.

lui-même aveuglément? Le temps cyclique et sans pitié? C'est à l'auditoire, à nous autres lecteurs d'en déduire la morale.

Voici le lion.[15] Il exprime par son comportement physique l'autorité et la force. Cela est bien évident. Et sans doute, ce souverain indomptable et parfois véhément correspond-il à la noblesse dans la hiérarchie sociale traditionnelle des peuples berbères. Le lion est intelligent et sa grandiose majesté le place d'emblée à un niveau supérieur quasi divin. N'oublions pas que Ali, le gendre de Mahommet, dont le nom est exalté par la secte des Shiites, est "le lion d'Allah."

Et le chacal, animal de mauvais augure avec sa longue queue touffue, ses grandes oreilles pointues et ses membres grêles ainsi que le décrit Taos Amrouche, il rôde autour des camps; il rôde avec entêtement autour de ses proies et de ses ennemis. Il est craint pour son avidité, pour sa colère féroce et sa vélocité agressive. Il se montre entièrement dépourvu de moralité et son aspect sinistre reflète son âme corrompue. Pour autant qu'un chacal puisse avoir une âme et une âme de surcroît corrompue!

On se rend compte de la distance que l'auteur établit entre les animaux tels qu'ils sont décrits et tels qu'ils sont dans la nature: il s'agit ici de dégager une morale en lui donnant corps concrêt. Cet éloignement, justement, rend l'impossible plausible.

Dans d'autre cas, pour les besoins de la cause, les perceptions populaires du monde physique alentour ne sont pas perturbées. Ainsi Taos Amrouche en appelle-t-elle aux perdrix,[16] aux douces perdrix qui, dans la poésie et la tradition kabyles, sonte le symbole de la grâce et de la beauté féminines. Nous les retrouvons donc avec ces mêmes attributs. Plus encore, elles ont maintenant le don de protéger et de venir en aide aux autres animaux qui se trouvent dans des situations périlleuses. Le lion, le puissant lion lui-même a recours à la miséricorde des perdrix. Il est d'autant plus intéressant de voir s'établir ici un lien entre deux espèces totalement séparés zoologiquement et symboliquement. Car enfin, voilà le roi des animaux, symbole de la force suprême, qui est secouru par de faibles volailles que le moindre bruit effraie.

Cela n'est pas sans nous rappeler la fable de La Fontaine, *Le lion et le rat*. Et l'implication, la morale, sont tout aussi claires et nettes chez l'auteur français et chez Taos Amrouche: on a souvent besoin d'un plus petit que soi. De nouveau, nous pouvons aussi bien faire un rapprochement avec un autre conte de Birago Diop, *Le taureau de Bouki*, bien que dans cette histoire nous assistions à un curieux prolongement de cette morale. En effet, le petit lapin se joue malicieusement de l'hyène qui est, par nature, stupide et de mauvaise foi.[17]

Autre personnage que "le vieux sage," vieillard sympathique que l'on honore et vénère. Sa longue expérience, sa sagesse et sa patience font de lui une sorte de divinité suprême qui est toujours disposée à écouter attentivement et à guider celui dont la détresse est profonde ou celui que la vie a égaré.

On ne peut bien sûr parler de personnages de contes sans mentionner les princes

[15] op. cit. "Histoire du vieux lion et du voil de perdrix," pp. 153-55.

[16] Ibid.

[17] Birago Diop, *Contes choisis*, pp. 144-54.

et les princesses qui abondent dans ce recueil. Le Prince Charmant et la Princesse Lointaine sont là pour nous faire rêver, pour nous sortir de la routine quotidienne grise et affligeante.[18] Ils représentent les vertus mêmes de l'adolescence, et ici de l'adolescence ''royale''. Le Prince est le héros jeune, rayonnant de joie et d'enthousiasme. Courageux, il surmonte les périls les plus dangereux; intrépide, il se lance dans les actions les plus extraordinaires; et tout cela pour mériter l'amour de la belle Princesse.

Celle-ci porte de magnifiques cheveux blonds (que cette blondeur suggère un désir ardent de soleil et de pureté offre peut'être d'intéressantes spéculations); chaste et vertueuse (en général, car nous avons vu une exception notable) et trouvera le bonheur idéal auprès du prince, compagnon fidèle.

Evidemment, le Prince et la Princesse sont l'idéalisation de l'Homme et de la Femme au pays de beauté, de jeunesse et d'amour — retour au Paradis Terrestre.

Dans certain contes, en dépit de sa vaillance, le Prince est victime de la sorcière Settoute que nous avons rencontrée il y a quelques instants. Cette vilaine créature change le Prince en monstre ou en animal, et il ne recouvre sa forme princière que sous l'effet d'un amour héroïque ou avec l'aide du Vieux Sage.

Ailleurs, par contre, le Prince orgueilleux est puni comme doit l'être l'orgueil. Lorsqu'il veut se mesurer à Dieu et devenir aussi puissant que celui-ci, tyrannisant ses sujets, le voici transformé en ''chat moche au pelage fauve'' qui sera persécuté par sa queue tout le restant de sa vie. Et puis, il perd son palais et la jouissance de toutes ses splendeurs.

Il reste deux personnages à traiter: l'enfant et Dieu, précisément. Ce sont là deux présences qui dominent tous les contes. L'enfant tel que le décrit Taos Amrouche est en quelque sorte un microcosme de la société dans laquelle il grandit et évolue. Ainsi nous le voyons tour à tour, et selon les circonstances très variées dans lesquelles il se trouve, affectueux, malin, espiègle, féroce, jaloux, menteur, paresseux — enfin, tout ce que nous connaissons chez les petits et chez les grands aussi bien! Il faut se dire que l'enfant compte énormément dans cette société qui lui doit survie et renouvellement.

Quant à Dieu, chez un peuple dont la mentalité est impregnée de religion, dont chaque acte journalier est un acte que prend sa mesure devant et dans le divin, il est bien évident que son omniprésésence et son omnipotence ne pouvaient manquer au déroulement des histoires que nous raconte Taos Amrouche. On le voit ici bienveillant ''Le Sultan put bénir Dieu qui avait créé si surprenante beauté,''[20] là généreux ''....jamais ils n'avaient vu pareille richesse octroyée par Dieu.''[21] mais aussi, à l'occasion, Dieu justicier et impitoyable envers les méchants ''La justice impitoyable de Dieu ferait la lumière.'' Et puis, quand Dieu tarde à se manifester, le croyant en appelle directement à lui, le sommant d'agir pour redresser les torts; c'est ainsi qu'un homme lésé maudit son adversaire en attirant les foudres divines

---

[18] Taos Amrouche, *Le grain magique*, ''La princess Soumicha,'' pp. 65-75; ''Roundja...'' pp. 181-199; etc.

[19] op. cit. p. 181.

[20] op. cit. p. 183.

[21] op. cit. p. 101.

sur sa tête: "Que Dieu te trahisse comme tu m'as trahi!"[22] Nous notons que Dieu se déclare souvent et décide alors d'envoyer un de ses lieutenants, un archange généralement, sur terre pour remettre les hommes dans le droit chemin ou, si besoin est, pour les punir de façon exemplaire.

Dieu, les enfants, les princes et princesses, le Vieux Sage, le lion, les perdrix, et bien d'autres encore, sont là pour étayer les contes certes, pour leur donner une matérialité tangible et facilement discernable, pour leur assurer pérennité. Mais aussi, ces personnages soulignent, accentuent le caractère didactique des contes; ce caractère que la tradition conserve précieusement et que chaque conteur se doit de perpétuer.

Car il faut sans cesse l'affirmer et ne pas l'oublier: c'est de la tradition, et de la tradition orale de surcroît, que Taos Amrouche extrait ses contes. Qu'elle les ait rendus si vivants, qu'elle ait su garder leurs qualités authentiques et toute leur valeur morale, est du à son talent de narratrice, à un style unique et parfaitement approprié pour cette tâche.

C'est justement cet aspect de l'oeuvre qu'il faudrait maintenant étudier un peu.

"Que mon conte soit beau et se déroule comme un long fil" est la formule initiale, la phrase magique que prononçait la mère de Taos Amrouche (Fadhma Amrouche) quand elle se mettait à raconter les histoires de son pays à ses enfants. Sa fille a gardé précieusement, reliqieusement même, cette petite phrase afin, dit-elle dans son introduction, de nous "faire pénétrer comme par magie dans l'univers de la légende.[24]

De même, elle a utilisé la formule finale qu'employait aussi sa mère "Mon conte est comme un ruisseau, je l'ai conté à des Seigneurs," pour conclure, signifiant par là (et je cite Taos Amrouche) "que le conte devait passer en nous comme un ruisseau, en enchantant pour toujours, et poursuivre sa course de bouche en bouche et d'âme en âme, jusqu'à la fin des temps."[25]

Le procédé, en lui-même, n'est pas nouveau et se retrouve dans toutes les littératures de tradition orale depuis Le Roman de Tristan et Iseut ("Seigneurs, vous plaît-il d'entendre un beau conte d'amour et de mort?" — "Seigneurs, les bons trouvères d'antan, Beroul et Thomas, et monseigneur Eilhart et maitre Gottfried, ont conté ce conte pour tous ceux qui aiment, non pour les autres,") aux récits que font les griots africains ou malgaches (notons en particulier chez ces derniers l'obligatoire miala-tsiny, sorte d'excuse et de compliment, au commencement de la narration).

Toujours est-il que ces deux formules sont très efficaces dans les contes de Taos Amrouche car nous savons de suite que nous allons pouvoir nous évader et nous laisser mener avec délices là où la narratrice veut nous conduire. Entre ces formules se déroulent les histoires décrites de façon singulière, chacune possédant son caractère propre et enrichie de dialogues très vifs et vivants.

---

[22] op. cit. p. 125.

[23] op. cit. p. 125.

[24] op. cit. p. 9.

[25] op. cit. pp. 10.

La narration nous présente en situation — dans un sens très existentialiste — le développment des évênements et des personnages qui les animent. En général, les descriptions sont sobres, claires, et parfois rudes comme les montagnes kabyles elles-mêmes. Il est évident que cette sobriété et cette simplicité correspondent au caractère foncièrement ''naturel'' sinon primitif (dans le meilleur sens du terme) des audiences auxquelles s'adressent les contes. Mais nous savons fort bien qu'il s'agit là de l'essence même du conte qui se doit d'aller droit au but sans les artifices qui entourent parfois d'autres genres littéraires. Ne s'agit-il pas en effet d'un acte dramatique auquel toute l'audience prend part active?

Et justement, c'est là qu'intervient le dialogue qui est mené tout au long de ces contes avec vivacité. On y reconnait le talent de l'écrivain qui a su reproduire l'art du conteur oral. Admirons par exemple tel dialogue tiré du conte *Histoire de la grenouille*[26] ou les personnages sont des êtres bien campés qui affirment leur individualité dans un échange bien enlevé.

> ''Le roitelet enfin se présente:
> — Qu'as-tu, mon oncle le Crapaud? Pourquoi cet air désespéré?
> — C'est la jouvencelle du jouvenceau qui s'est enfuie dans la mare et m'a laissé. Plusieurs ont essayé de me la ramener. Mais elle ne leur a pas fait bon visage.
> — Tu verras, moi, elle me suivra, car je ne la prierai pas.
> — Qui cogne à mon nid? Des débris tombent sur mon dîner!
> — C'est ton Seigneur le Roitelet des roitelets, vert comme le fiel. Tu vas marcher devant moi, ou gare à la matraque!
> — Un instant que je me pomponne! Un peu de rouge aux levres, un peu de noir aux yeux, et je te précede mon seigneur!''

Et nous autres auditeurs, par la magie de ce dialogue, nous entrons dans la création de conte. L'experience est à la fois exaltante et salutaire car nous sommes en fait devant un petit miroir, mais miroir tout de même où *nous ne pouvons pas ne pas nour voir!*

Mentionnons aussi en passant, et pris un peu au hasard, quelques-uns des traits qui dénotent la maîtrise artistique de Taos Amrouche.

Les descriptions de la nature, on doit s'y attendre, sont très nombreuses. Elles sont neessaires puisque les contes s'adressent après tout à des villageois constamment en contact avec leurs terres, leurs forêts, le climat et les animaux qu'ils rencontrent journellement. Ces descriptions dépassent souvent le simple effet visuel, le simple agrément esthétique. L'auteur en grand artiste donne à la nature un caractère spécial qui la rapproche des hommes. Ainsi cette amusante symbiose que nous trouvons dan l'extrait suivant: ''Pour fair honneur au Chat-pèlerin, les rats revêtirent leurs vêtements les plus beaux: gandouras blanches, burnous du Djérid. Ils se coiffèrent de hauts turbans et chaussèrent leurs souliers les plus neufs. Les souris, elles, se fardèrent avec soin: elles rougirent leurs lèvres à l'écorce de noyer. Elles se mirent du noir aux yeux, du rose aux joues...''[27]

Nous sommes bien dans le domaine de la magie et du fantastique, et nous avons

---

[26] op. cit pp. 34-35.

[27] op. cit. p. 211-212.

noté combien la réalité et la couleur locale y sont présentes. Les termes gandouras, burnous, turbans djellabah (des effets vestimentaires) lient la fantaisie et la réalité, l'invraisemblable et le possible. Plus encore, nous avons sans doute remarqué ''le turban vert''; or le vert est la couleur de l'Islam et représente ici subconsciemment l'enracinement des contes dans la mentalité locale.

On pourrait même affirmer que l'emploi de ce vocabulaire local ou la mention d'un trait culturel que nous connaissons nous associe magiquement c'est le cas de le dire, aux auditoires de jadis assemblés autour de la mère de Taos Amrouche, aux auditoires à naître aussi.

Art du conteur! Art de l'auteur!

Et de-ci de-là le suspens habilement maintenu, les déclarations ou les souhaits qui agrémentent traditionnellement la conversation, les expressions spontanées de joie et de tristesse dans ce monde de lumière et d'ombre fortes, attestent assez le talent de Taos Amrouche.

Pour terminer, notons la resurgence constante du nombre sept. Ceci n'est ici qu'une remarque mais qui ne manque pas d'étonner. Car enfin, voici sept frères,[28] sept Notables,[29] le septième étage du palais,[30] sept filles,[31] sept serpents,[32] sept jours et sept muits,[33] le dragon-aux-sept-têtes,[34] et ainsi de suite.

Le nombre sept, nous le savons, porte en soi valeur symbolique; il est sans cesse invoqué dans notre culture judéo-chrétienne; il était caractéristique du culte d'Apollon, et on le rencontre aussi bien en Chine traditionnelle que chez les Mayas d'Amérique Centrale. En Islam, il est également un nombre faste, symbole de perfection — non seulement les sept cieux ou sept portes, mais aussi rappelons que lors du pélérinage à La Mecque les fidelles doivent effectuer sept tours de la Kaaba.

Que dire ou que déduire de cette récurrence? C'est là sans doute object à spéculations intéressantes qui demandent une autre étude. Terminons donc celle-ci selon la formule traditionnelle: ''Mon conte est comme un ruisseau, je l'ai conté à des Seigneurs.''[35]

[28] op. cit. p. 119.

[29] op. cit. p. 198.

[30] op. cit. p. 89.

[31] op. cit. 168.

[32] op. cit. p. 145.

[33] op. cit. p. 89.

[34] op. cit. p. 88.

[35] cf. fin de tous les contes.

THE EAST

THE EAST

A BASIC ANATOMY
OF EAST AFRICAN LITERATURE

Bernth Lindfors
University of Texas, Austin

East African literature in English has grown as much by a process of steady accretion as by a dymanic dialectic of mutation, with each fresh thrust moving in a direction counter to that of its immediate predecessor, even when preoccupied with similar thematic concerns. Although the changes in this swelling body of literature have been striking and swift, several threads of continuity have held the corpus together, giving it a semblance of organic interrelatedness and orderly development despite periodic ruptures and dislocations. Indeed, the unpredictability of East African literature has been one of its greatest strengths, for it has forced readers to reassess old truths from new vantage points. Diversity, instead of leading to framentation, has contributed a measure of coherent articulation to this young literature.

The first major step in East African literature was taken by Ngugi wa Thiong'o when he wrote *The River Between* (1965) and *Weep Not, Child* (1964), historical novels recreating Gikuyu experience during colonial times. Like Chinua Achebe a few years earlier, Ngugi wated to use his fiction to rewrite African history from an African perspective. He spoke of the African novelist being "haunted by a sense of the past. His work is often an attempt to come to terms with 'the thing that has been,' a struggle, as it were, to sensitively register his encounter with history, his people's history."[1] This was important work to do in the years immediately preceding and following independence, for in coming to terms with the past, the writer was helping his fellow Kenyans to understand and evaluate what had happened to them during the colonial era. The writer, in other words, was functioning as a nationlist historian, a chronicler with a patriotic message. He wrote in order to educate and raise the political consciousness of his people.

Ngugi has continued producing this kind of didactic fiction even while writing of more contemporary times. His later novels, *A Grain of Wheat* (1967) and *Petals of Blood* (1977), are set in post-independence Kenya, but they reach back into the past in order to cxplain the present. In an interview published shortly after *Petals of Blood* had appeared, Ngugi said, "I look at contemporary society but in a historical perspective. I examine the different social forces that are encroaching on the minds and lives of Kenyan people today and also their historical roots...a glance at contemporary society has been at the same time a glance at our history."[2] The moral seriousness of this diachronic vision of Kenyan society has been one of the hallmarks of Ngugi's fiction. He is a sober social critic who believes that literature should carry a profound political message.

---

[1] Ngugi wa Thiong'o, *Homecoming: Essays on African and Caribbean Literature, Culture and Politics* (London: Heinemann, 1972), p. 39.

[2] " 'Open Criticism is Very Health in Any Society...'," *Sunday Nation* (Nairobi), 17 July 1977, p. 10.

The second major writer to emerge in East Africa was Okot p'Bitek, whose *Song of Lawino* (1966) quickly established his reputation as a lyric poet. p'Bitek went on to write three more book-length "songs" — *Song of Ocol* (1970), *Song of Prisoner* (1971), and *Song of Malaya* (1971) — all of them following the formula that had proven so successful in his first venture into verse. The most remarkable feature of p'Bitek's writing was that it was humorous without being frivolous. The gentle, genial satire in his songs made readers laugh but also made them think.

What p'Bitek wanted Africans to think about was their own cultural identity. He was dismayed when he saw educated Africans rejecting their traditional culture and trying to imitate Western ways. Such "apemanship" was the primary target of his satire in *Song of Lawino* and *Song of Ocol*, and even when he turned to larger socio-political themes in his later songs, he was still concerned with mocking the absurdities arising out of cultural confusion. His aim was to effect a "cultural revolution," which he defined as a "revolt against Western cultural domination (and) a flowering of African creativity."[3] In an interview he said:

> All my writings, whether they are anthropological monographs, studies of religion, essays, songs, poems, or even traditional stories and proverbs such as I am collecting now, all of them are ammunition for one big battle: the battle to decide where we here in Africa are going and what kind of society we are building. I think you will find great similarities in all the different things I have been producing because they all have basically the same aim.[4]

Yet when singing, p'Bitek's voice carried a bit further because there was laughter embedded in the song — laughter tinged with sorrow. p'Bitek's great contribution to East African literature was his distinctive blend of hilarious but thoughtful cultural satire. He too wanted to get a message across to his people, but he chose a different medium to convey his ideas.

The third major figure on the East African literary scene was Taban lo Liyong, whose impact is more difficult to define because it has taken so many shapes and forms. Unlike Ngugi and p'Bitek, Liyong has not specialized in one genre of writing but has experimented with various types of fiction, poetry, essays and aphorisms. Although his wit can be quite amusing, his pronouncements refreshingly unconventional, and his posture boldly iconoclastic, he has not made his greatest contribution in the realm of ideas. Indeed, sometimes he contradicts himself by arguing on too many sides of an issue. He freely admits this, insisting that he shouldn't be held responsible today for statements he made yesterday, when he was an altogether different person.[5] One must not expect consistency from a human being so responsive to the dynamics of change.

Yet it is Liyong's restless quest for creative self-expressions that is his most remarkable quality. He does not like to repeat himself so he seeks new ways of saying things. He once stated:

[3] Okot p'Bitek, *Africa's Cultural Revolution* (Nairobi: Macmillan, 1973), p. 17.

[4] Bernth Lindfors, "An Interview with Okot p'Bitek," *World Literature Written in English*, 16 (1977), 291-92.

[5] See, e.g., *Meditations of Taban lo Liyong* (London: Rex Collings, 1978), pp. 45-47.

> When I started writing my essays, each essay was different from the others. There was also a variety of styles for the short stories in *Fixions* and *The Uniformed Man*. All of them were different. I don't know whether readers have actually found that out: no story is told exactly as the previous one was. It was like saying, "Okay, future East African writers, here are a variety of forms. Choose the ones you like; choose the mode of writing you prefer." That was the type of thing I was trying to do.[6]

In other words, what matters most to a writer such as Liyong is originality of form and style. The message is less important than the medium. Unlike Ngugi and p'Bitek, Liyong is interest primarily in creating art for art's sake.

The next writer to make a major impression on the East African literary scene was Charles Mangua, whose episodic potboilers *Son of Woman* (1971) and *A Tail in the Mouth* (1972) appeared in the early 1970's. These novels made publishing history by quickly outselling all previous works of fiction produced in East Africa. *Son of Woman* went through three printings in its first year, and *A Tail in the Mouth* sold equally well and was one of the first books to be awarded the Jomo Kenyatta Prize for Literature. This was truly popular diction, and the extent of Mangua's influence on East African literature can be measured by the number of pop novels of the same type that were published in Kenya in the years immediately following.

Son of Woman was a racy, picaresque tale about the son of a prostitute who tried to make his way through life by cleverly deceiving his fellow man and regularly seducing fallen women. Though it has been termed "a work of erotic realism,"[7] *Son of Woman* really belongs in the "ha-ha" school of soft pornography. Mangua, through the antics of a fallible, oversexed hero, was simply trying to entertain his readers with an extraordinary chain of comic copulations.

The same triviality of purpose can be found in *A Tail in the Mouth*, which goes a step beyond its predecessor in cynicism by subjecting hallowed nationalistic notions to ridicule. For instance, in surveying East African society with a sardonic eye, Mangua ventures to poke fun at the Mau Mau freedom fighters, offering almost a parody of the kind of somber historical fiction that Ngugi was bent on creating. Mangua's irreverence is enjoyable, but it is almost impossible to find a stable moral center in the chaotic flux of his narrative. He seems content to settle for a quick chuckle here and there, never striving to sustain a consistent ironic outlook on the confused society he portrays. He writes for the gut rather than the head or the heart.

An even less cerebral author, who emerged in Kenya shortly after Mangua's sensational debut, dominated the East African literary scene in the mid-1970's. This was David Maillu, who first self-published mini-novels *Unfit for Human Consumption* (1973) and *Troubles* (1974) as well as his books of p'Bitek-like poetry *My Dear Bottle* (1973) and *After 4:30* (1973), sold so well that he was able to launch his own publishing firm, Comb Books, on the proceeds. He claims not to

[6] Interview with Taban lo Liyong recorded by Bernth Lindfors, 30 December 1976.

[7] Peter Nazareth, *Literature and Society in Modern Africa* (Nairobi: East African Literature Bureau, 1972), p. 185.

have imitated p'Bitek's style of singing,[8] but certainly he made a wise commercial decision to opt for a poetic idiom that had already proven remarkably popular in East Africa. His fiction tended to focus on the lives of office workers in Nairobi — bosses, clerks, secretaries, and other denizens of the bureaucracy. All these early works attracted numerous readers. Indeed, nearly every new Comb Book with Maillu's name on the cover — even those written by other authors — became an instant best-seller. When asked what account for the wide appeal of his works, Maillu replied:

> People say that I hit the nail on the head, whatever that means. People say that they see themselves when they are reading the books; they can identify with situations and characters. Basically, I think there are three things that tend to make the books popular. Humour is one, frankness may be another, and some people say the books contain wisdom, but I don't know what kind of wisdom that is.[9]

By "frankness" Maillu means sexual explicitness. In describing the zesty bedroom gymnastics of Nairobi's bureaucrats, Maillu even outstripped Mangua in sheer volume of salacious detail. Such frankness was part of his formula for publishing success. With Maillu, then, East African literature can be said to have reached an extreme of sexploitation and frivolity. The aim was more to titillate than to teach. The focus had now shifted from the gut to the groin.

A basic anatomy of East African literature representing the contributions made by these five key writers would look something like this:

Author	Primary interest	Primary intention	Major mode of expression	Anatomical analogy
Ngugi	historical/ political	instruction	serious fiction	head
p'Bitek	cultural	entertainment and instruction	satirical song	heart and lungs
Liyong	morphological	exploration	various experimental forms	skeletal and circulatory systems
Mangua	recreational	amusement	picaresque fiction	lower viscera
Maillu	commercial	sales	most popular forms: short fiction and long songs	groin

[8] Interview with David G. Maillu recorded by Bernth Lindfors, 4 August 1976.

[9] *Ibid.*

With this rudimentary anatomy in mind, it is possible to classify much of the English-language literature that has been produced in East Africa. Kenyan writers such as Godwin Wachira, John Karoki, Stephen Ngubiah, Charity Waciuma and Lydia Mumbi Nguya have reconstructed the Gikuyu past much as Ngugi did. Grace Okot, Khadambi Asalche, Kenneth Watene and Leonard Kibera of Kenya, Robert Serumaga and Peter Nazareth of Uganda, and Gabriel Ruhumbika and Ismael Mbise of Tanzania have treated serious historical or political themes in their writings, sometimes concentrating on the past, sometimes on the present. Ngugi has not been the only influence on such writers, but he was the first in East Africa to stake out the territory they have chosen to explore, so in a sense all of them can be regarded as descended from him.

The p'Bitek school of satirical song would include such poets of Joseph Buruga, Okello Oculi, and Cliff Lubwa p'Chong of Uganda and Muthoni Likimani of Kenya, all of whom have made use of long, mocking soliloquies in free verse to comment on indigenous socio-cultural phenomena. A recent example of prose in this mode would be Alumidi Asinya's *The Amazing Saga of Field Marshall Abdulla Salim Fisi* (1977), a beast fable about the career of Idi Amin; the Foreword to this book even recommends that authors try the ''mild, gentle way'' of getting a message across through laughter. This is precisely what Okot p'Bitek stands for.

It is more difficult to single out followers of Taban lo Liyong because any true believer in his doctrine of originality would have to pursue a path radically different from that of any predecessor, including Liyong. At least one literary critic has attempted to imitate his unorthodox, mind-jarring style,[10] but as Elimo Njau said some years ago, ''Copying puts God to sleep.''[11]

The only East African author who has come close to Liyong's trick of devising an entirely new literary form to carry the weight of unconventional thoughts is Ali Mazrui, whose ''novel of ideas,'' *The Trial of Christopher Okigbo* (1971), took the shape of a debate in an African afterworld. By adopting such a strategy of presentation, Mazrui could concentrate on courtroom polemics, examining a topical issue from antithetical points of view. What really matters in a structure of this sort is not who wins the case but how well the argument is conducted by each side. The experimental novelist has a particular medium to express, not a particular message.

The tradition of popular writing best emplified by the works of Charles Mangua was also established by a few novels that came out at about the same time as *Son of Woman* — specificially *The Experience* (1970) by Eneriko Seruma and *The People's Bachelor* (1972) by Austin Bukenya. One can see the works of Mwangi Ruheni and Samuel Kahiga as falling into the literary tradition as well, even though they lack Mangua's irreverent tone and preoccupation with sex and outrageous roguishness. All of them are light, episodic tales intended primarily for entertainment. Some of the innocuous pop novelettes published in the mid-1970's by Heinemann East Africa, Longman Kenya, and Transafrica Publishers could be put into this category, too.

---

[10] Gideon Mutiso, ''A Spastic Montage of the Intellectual Broker,'' *Busara*, 4, 1 (1972), 15-20.

[11] *Transition*, 9 (1963), 15.

The majority of David Maillu's proteges are authors published by Comb Books, and one wonders how much of a hand he may have had in shaping the books they wrote. For instance, Jasinta Mote's *The Flesh* (1975), supposedly the confessions of a prostitute, has emblazoned on its cover the words "produced by David G. Maillu," and Maillu admits in the Introduction to the book that he himself encouraged the author to write her story in their common mother tongue and then took it upon himself "to translate, assemble the many episodes scattered in a mass of writing, and try to construct a logical reading from it."[12] One wonders if he did the same with Maina Allan's *One by One* (1975) which was published "with a touch by David G. Maillu."[13] John Kibwana's *Utisi* (1974), Pal N. Njue's *My Lovely Mother* (1976), and Andrew M. Mwiwawi's *The Act* (1976), all published by Comb Books, do not carry such an inscription, but every one is written in Maillu's "frank" manner.

Maillu's influence can also be seen in the recent products of other publishing houses. Muli Mutiso's *Sugar Babies* (1975), Omunjakko Nakibimbiri's *The Sobbing Sounds* (1975), and Bingu Matata's sleazy *Love for Sale* (1975) and *Free Love* (1975) appear to have been published solely to capitalize on the trend toward sexually explicit popular literature. These books pander to the prurient interests of their readers, offering little more than an amusing succession of unusual orgasms. This is literary prostitution of the worst sort.

Occasionally is is possible to detect two of the major tendencies in East African literature in the work of a single author. Meja Mwangi, for example, wrote two novels, *Taste of Death* (1975) and *Carcase for Hounds* (1974), under the influence of Ngugi; both are heroic sagas set in the Mau Mau era. But in *Kill Me Quick* (1973) and *Going Down River Road* (1976) Mwangi turned to modern urban life and told episodic adventure stories that border on the picaresque; although these works are still fairly serious in tone, they show definite signs of moving toward a more popular idiom.

Moreover, the fact that Ngugi himself structured his most recent novel *Petals of Blood* as a murder mystery may indicate that he too is now seeking to reach the widest possible audience, a mass audience that appreciates formula fiction. In the future one should perhaps expect to see more such mutations grow out of the interaction between different literary impulses in East Africa.

Any attempt to trace the evolution of East African literature in English must recognize the account for its growing tendency toward popularization. Some might see this as a sign of the premature decline of a new literary civilization, others as an encouraging indication that more East Africans are reading today than every before. In constructing a basic anatomy of this literature we have sought only to place the major organic parts in relationship to one another. The delineation of the rest of the corpus — including limbs, warts, hair and other noteworthy extrusions — will have to await a fuller post-mortem examination. In the meantime East African literature will no doubt continue to grow, surprising us with its unexpected twists and turns that in retrospect will seem almost inevitable. Living

[12] Jasinta Mote, *The Flesh* (Nairobi: Comb Books, 1975), p. 11.

[13] Front cover of Maina Allan, *One by One* (Nairobi: Comb Books, 1975).

organisms have a tendency to develop selectively, realizing their full potential in certain areas but failing to extend themselves significantly in others. Finding an adequate explanation for this idiosyncratic pattern of growth and development is the challenge of future scholarship.

NG'OMBE AKIVUNDIKA GUU..: PRELIMINARY REMARKS ON THE PROVERB-STORY IN WRITTEN SWAHILI LITERATURE

F.E.M.K. Senkoro
University of Dar es Salaam

Introduction

Although much has been written concerning Swahili proverbs, there has been little commentary on the use of the proverbs by Swahili prose fiction writers. One of the earliest efforts to deal with the subject of Swahili proverbs was by W.E. Taylor, who in 1891 made a collection of a number of Swahili proverbs. The collection was published much later, in 1924, under the title *African Aphorisms, or Saws From Swahili Land*.[1] The attitude of merely collecting the proverbs without giving them a deep, scholarly analysis has continued up to the present day. The most recent works on proverbs and sayings from Tanzania[2] jointly written by C.K. Omari, W.D. Kamera and E. Kezilahabi illustrate this fact. Although the works give us quite a thought-provoking collection of proverbs and sayings, and try hard to offer some contextual explanations, often the endeavours only skim superficial moral interpretations from the proverbs and sayings, neglecting their depths of ambiguity, irony, and allusion.

In one of her works on African oral literature[3] Ruth Finnegan barely mentions how written forms in Africa sometimes make use of "traditional proverbs," she makes a quick and poorly elaborated reference to the poems by the famous East African poet, Muyaka bin Haji.

Lyndon Harries' work on the subject,[4] and Jan Knappert's examine primarily non-literary aspects of the proverbs, paying no heed to their use in written Swahili literature.

Carolyn A. Parker has worked widely on Swahili proverbs, although also not specifically on the distinct application of the proverbs in written Swahili prose fiction.[6] Most of her surveys are much more informed than many other works on the subject to date. They aid in viewing the proverbs as a social phenomenon and, thus, in understanding their contexts and social significance.

---

[1] (London: Sheldon Press, 1924 (first printed 1884).)

[2] C.K. Omari et al., *Methali na Misemo kutoka Tanzania*: 1 & 2 (Nairobi: East African Literature Bureau, 1977 and 1978 respectively).

[3] Ruth Finnegan, *Oral Literature in Africa* (London: Oxford, 1971).

[4] "African Proverbs: The Problem of Identification," in W.L. Ballard, ed., *Essays on African Literature* (Atlanta: School of Arts and Sciences, Georgia State University, 1973), pp. 89-96.

[5] "Rhyming Swahili Proverbs," and "Swahili Proverb Songs," in *Africa and Ubersee*, 49 (1966), pp. 100-112 and 59 (1976), pp. 107-112 respectively.

[6] See the list of her works in the Bibliography below.

One detailed and interesting work on the subject is Kofi Osare Opoku's *Speak to the Winds: Proverbs from Africa*, which examines a wide range of proverbs as well as their social context and significance in the lives of the African peoples.

Carol M. Eastman's article, "The Proverb in Modern Writtern Swahili Literature: An Aid to Proverb Elicitation"[7] is one of the very few works which deal with the application and effect of proverbs on Swahili fiction. This attempt, however, despite its good intentions, does not always provide sufficient assistance in the task of eliciting and understanding both the literary works and the proverbs. It is a hasty and sketchy work. In some instances its generalizations and misinformation are both confounding and astonishing.[8] Eastman in this article, attempts to show how three contemporary Swahili authors (Ebrahim Hussein, Graham Hyslop and Gerishon Ngugi) have interwoven "Folk Art" with their works via proverbs. She illustrates how such works have provided contextual explanations of the writers' peoples' sayings. One would expect the venture to offer a deep and critical analysis of the texts in the light of, hopefully, a profound understanding of the Swahili proverbs. Eastman, however, merely examines their exterior moral quality, and this superficial treatment results eventually in the "creation" of a distorted Swahili proverb. In the last analysis, the whole exercise shows the limitations of hearsay as a basis for criticism.[9]

This short survey of literature shows that although much has been done there is still much more to be desired, starting on the simple level of mere preliminary examination of the proverbs. And when one looks at what has been done it becomes obvious that a deeper and more detailed analysis of the Swahili proverbs yets needs to be made. The poverty in the general analysis of the proverbs can perhaps account for the lack of critical sophistication in the scholarship of the application of proverbs in Swahili literature.

This paper will attempt to investigate how some written Swahili short stories and novels are built exclusively on the essence of a single, yet unifying proverb. In so doing, it will focus on the proverbs as channels not only for the moral, but also,

---

[7] In Richard M. Dorson, ed., *African Folklore* (Bloomington and London: Indiana University Press, 1972), pp. 193-209.

[8] For example, concerning the proverb "Panapo nia ipo njia" ("Where there is will there is a way," p. 203), Eastman gives her informers' interpretation and generalizes it to be the "Swahili Sense" of the proverb. Ironically enough, the conventional meaning of the proverb, which implies encouragement and perseverance — that whenever a person what to do or get something in earnest he can always find a way to do/get it, provided he has strong will and determination — is paraphrased and claimed to be Eastman's. Worst of them all is the strangely coined "Dua la mwewe halimpatii kuku" (p. 204) instead of the correct Swahili one, "Dua la kuku halimpati mwewe." It is unpardonable the way the word *halimpati* has been given the same meaning as *halimpatii* — two very different words with very different meanings. The correct Swahili version of the proverb translates roughly as "The curse of the chicken (after its chicks have been snatched by the hawk) doesn't affect the hawk." Although it can be given some other moralistic meanings, this proverb is one of those which have often been used by exploiters to justify their "right" to exploit and oppress others.

[9] Footnote 8 above applies. Although so much can be said and elaborated by numerous examples drawn from works of many other archair-expatriate "critics" some of whom have been misnamed "experts of Swahili and Tanzanian Literature," more evidence is beyond the scope of the present paper.

and more importantly, for the satirical-political messages — a function of proverbs often overlooked by scholars. The paper will also discuss the significance of such artistic use of proverbs in Swahili literature.

Moralistic Proverb-Stories and Their Ideological Implications

Charlton Laird, in his *Webster's New World Thesaurus*, gives as some of the synonyms for proverb, works like "moral" and "folk wisdom" (p. 352). The Herskovits[10] regard proverbs as fountains of "insight into behaviour," and they talk at length on the "grammar of values" — moral values — to be found in proverbs. C.H. Holman in his *A Handbook to Literature*, says that proverbs are shrewd observations about practical life, and that these observations are ultimately full of "wisdom."

The tendency to emphasize the moralistic aspect of proverbs when interpreting stories that use proverbs as their basis is widespread in criticism of Swahili literature. This paper regards such a tendency as a major weakness, and will demonstrate a more fruitful alternative approach in the interpretation of proverb-stories.

In J.K. Kiimbila's collection of short stories entitled *Visa Vya Walimwengu* (*"What a World!"*), proverb stories with proverbs as their titles, such as "'Yote Yang'aayo Usidhani ni Dhahabu" ("All that glitters is not gold"), "Mchimba Kisimahuingia mwenyewe" ("He who digs a well falls into it himself"), "Akili ni Nywele, kila mtu ana Zake" ("Cleverness is similar to hair, everybody has his own"), "Mali Bila Daftari Hupotea Bila Habari" ("Business lacking in account keeping goes bankrupt unnoticed"), "Meno Meupe Roho Nyeusi" ("White teeth black heart") and "Asiyesikia la Mkuu Huvunyika Guu" ("He who does not heed his elder's advice gets a broken leg") — all these have one major aim: to "teach" people how to behave by preaching about life. In "Yote Yang'aayo Usidhani ni Dhahabu" for example, we are told not to judge each other merely by external appearances. Saida, a young and beautiful secondary school girl, falls in love with Deogratius. She goes to live with him as his wife simply because of the expensive borrowed suit that he is wearing and because it successfully deceives her into believing that Deo's master's huge mansion is his. In the end, when the truth is revealed Deo runs away from Saida, who then has to go back to her parents. The moral of the story, as the title suggests, is that "all that glitters is not gold."

We also see the moralistic duty of the proverb-story in the *Hadithi za Kusisimua* ("Titillating stories") series (published by Longman Kenya between 1968 and 1972). In thi short-lived series of "popular" novelettes dealing with "crime and passion" one encounters such proverbial titles as Omolo's *Mtaka Yote Hukosa Yote* (1968), *Mwerevu Hajinyoi* (1971), and *Uhalifu Haulipi* (1971). In all these stories there are characters who, for no apparent reason, turn into "bad" people — unfit to live among "good," "clean" citizens. In *Mtaka Yote Hukosa Yote* ("He who wants all loses all"), Juma, an up-and-coming Luhya man who has been realized in a "good Christian way" turns into a great thief and drunkard in the

[10] Melville J. and Frances S. Herskovits, *Dahomean Narratives: A Cross Cultural Analysis* (Evanston, Illinois, 1956), p. 56.

cities of Thika and Nairobi. He is finally caught and, *of course*, jailed. The moral "whoever wants all loses all" is thus illustrated. In this way, a poor and hungry man, in taking a loaf of bread reserved for a dog is condemned for "wanting all," while the greed of the rich — seen as legitimate — is taken for granted.

In *Uhalifu Haulipi* ("Crime does not pay"), Okelo, kicked out of school, moves from his village of Got-Rateng to Kisumu, and finally to Nairobi where the turns into a "thief." He is inevitably caught by the ever-present police, and is sentenced to a ten-year imprisonment and twenty four lashes. Supposedly embarrassed by the presence of his family at the trial and by the nature of the punishment, Okelo is made to regret his wicked ways by the author who, no doubt, rejoices in sharing with the audience the moral that "crime does not pay."

A similar plot operates in *Mwerevu Hajinyoi* ("A clever man does not shave himself"). Here, John Apu Mageta moves from Kisumu to Nairobi, He is then involved in a life of "crime" which inevitably draws him to a six-year prison sentence accompanied by twelve lashes on his bare buttocks.

The list of stories in this vein could be increased tenfold. However, for the present purpose the above will serve as very good examples of the nature and function of moralistic proverb-stories in Swahili literature.

These stories touch on various issues, often very sensitive and burning, concerning the realities of life in the writers' societies. However, after touching on vital issues, the stories retreat from a much needed in-depth examination. In many instances, the authors of the proverb stories use the moral ideology inherent in their works to distract the attention of the readers from the true nature of important issues in society. The stories of the *crime-does-not-pay* type for example, can be said to deliberately encourage wrong attitudes towards the problems facing poor people today. Through the use of the coercive force of oppressive state power, poor people — unfairly labelled "criminals" — are caught by the police and jailed. While in prison, these people are lashed and whipped, and this is called straightening the criminal into a good citizen. This crime against people is done under the guise of the moral of *"crime does not pay."*

These moralistic "crime" and "passion" stories, like the Swahili detective novels,[11] do not make any attempt to look into the root causes of the crimes. To Kiimbila in "Yote Yang'aayo Usidhani ni Dhahabu," for example, it does not seem to matter so much that there are poor Deo's in the writer's society, who, like dogs, have to obey their masters. It does not seem to matter that the people are forced to keep their masters' houses clean, and at the same time have to sweat endlessly in the latters' farms so as to get meagre pay which is not even enough to buy a wedding suit. The issues dealt with in these stories are unavoidably class issues which are ultimately tied to the ownership of the means of production in

[11] For an interesting, though not thorough, account of the Swahili detective novels, see E. Kezilahabi, "Riwaya az Kiswahili za Upeleleza," in *Kiswahili*, Vol. 45(2) (1973), pp. 36-40.

Also Penina Muhando and Ndyanao Balisidya give an interesting view on the topic in their *Fasihi na Sanaa za Maonyesho* (Dar es Salaam: Tanzania Publishing House, 1976), pp. 68-72.

I have dealt with the subject too in my University of Dar es Salaam M.A. (Fasihi) Thesis, "Riwaya ya Kiswahili na Maendeleo ya Umma" (forthcoming, Dar es Salaam: Dar es Salaam University Press, 1981); and in my "Remarks on Current Ideological trends in the Swahili Novel," in *African Studies Association Archives 1978* (University of California, Los Angeles; A.S.A., 1978).

society, and also to the operations of the capitalist system. Omolo's stories portray the city as a force which breeds crime. They do not, however, go deeper than this surface. The moral ideology in proverbs in the treatment of social issues is not sufficiently influential in changing the vile system of capitalism which is the real enemy of the down-trodden people.

I therefore disagree with Carolyn Parker and Douglas F. Kavugha's contention that the novelettes in *Hadithi za Kusisimua* series "are not vehicles for political expression."[12] Quite the contrary. These novelettes are used as intensive political propaganda; they are utilized to create a false image of the reality and the nature of the so-called "crimes." Through this misrepresentation the works are supposed to create the illusion that poor people are inherently bad, and that whenever they indulge in "criminal" life, the only solution is for the armed servants of the capitalist order to catch them, jail them and bombard them with torrents of moralizing on how "crime does not pay."

The whole essence of these moralistic "crime" and "passion" tales is idealism, and it is this that the propagators of such tales want to spread among the people. Thus, contrary to the analysis given by Parker and Kavugha, which alleges that in these stories "the heroes...help bring the forces of evil to justice,"[13] the truth is that the forces of evil and oppression in these stories intimidate people in the false name of justice and peace. These proverb-stories, by depending on moralistic preachings as the "solutions" to the so-called evils, deny the possibility of or even belief in real social change and victory for the people.

What then, can we conclude concerning this kind of literature? What I have said elsewhere about the Swahili detective novel[14] applies squarely here and should be repeated:

> These stories, ultimately, try to parade and create fear in people, the fear of the "omnipotence" of the fascist power of the neo-colonial petit-bourgeois state — the police, the so-called courts of law, prisons and so on. In this trend people are lured into confusions concerning the real state of affairs in society. Through the so-called "defeat of the culprits," people are urged to humble themselves and kneel impotently before their master, never questioning the source of the massive wealth owned by those in power. It is preached to them that they should live "decent" lives of peaceful law-abiding citizens in the midst of poverty while a few people live in luxury (p. 12).

Through a careful analysis, one soon discovers the idological significance of these stories, and the socio-politico-economic system for which the ideology in the stories is functioning. These stories constitute in Swahili literature a trend that attempts to hang veils between social consciousness and the material world. They

---

[12] Carolyn A. Parker and Douglas F. Kavugha, "Hadithi za Kusisimua: Crime and Passion in Swahili Literature," paper presented at the African studies Association Meeting, Houston, November 1977, obtainable from the A.S.A., University of California, Los Angeles.

[13] Ibid.

[14] See "Remarks on Current Ideological Trends in the Swahili Novel," *African Studies Association Archives 1978* (University of California, Los Angeles; A.S.A., 1978).

tell the all too familiar lie of a utopian world in which the mere stating of a proverb is capable of changing a poor man into a "good" subject — in other words into a "rich" citizen — while he continues to wallow in poverty and humiliation ("rich" being, of course, a capitalist synonym for "good"). The fact that the trend of such publications was short-lived is very revealing in itself. People read the stories which much enthusiasm at the beginning, thus causing several critics' itching pens to jump immediately to misuse the word "popular" in describing the stories.[15] Within no time at all, the poeple rejected the stories. In effect these stories can never be popular in the long run. People want to read how they can bring about meaningful changes to their present lives. They want to know how they can win victory in their war against poverty, disease, ignorance and, above all, exploitation of man by man. It is no wonder, then, that the *Hadithi za Kusisimua* series and similar collections steeped in illusions have a very short-lived popularity.

The Satirical-Political Aspect in Proverb-Stories

Satire informs a large number of proverbs in most cultures. Such satire could be aimed at other races (especially in a colonial situation), at rival "localities," at opposing classes in society, and so on. I wish to point out this important aspect of proverbs by examining two main works in Swahili literature: Shaaban Robert's *Kusadikika*, and a short story, "Wali wa Ndevu," by Tilumanya, from Gabriel Ruhumbika, ed., *Parapanda*.

Among the critics of Shaaban Robert's *Kusadikika* ("Kusadikika: A country of Believers"), none seems to have analysed the proverb, "Ng'ombe akivunjika mguu malishoni hujikokota zizini kusaidiwa," which Shaaban Robert has chosen to quote even before the opening of this novel. It roughly translates "When a cow gets hurt while grazing, it limps home for help." Another version of the proverb, which uses the exotic Mwambao Swahili, is "Ng'ombe akivundika guu hukimbilia zizini." Among the Asu people in North-Eastern Tanzania there is a similar version which would, however, roughly translate thus: "When a cow gets hurt while grazing, it limps home so that its wound may be licked be fellow cows." We shall use both versions of the proverb in our analysis, for they are of the same root.

This proverb plays a very important role in the story of the country of Kusadikika. The whole novel is built on the essence of this single proverb, and certainly the author intended his readers to focus their attention on this fact. The role of this proverb in *Kusadikika* however, is a double one having a surface and a hidden meaning. The surface message deals with the moral of the proverb which, as Carolyn Parker has put it, is that one must go to the proper place for help when one is in trouble. Nonetheless, the deeper implications of a proverb can, at times, counter the whole essence of the surface meaning. Shaaban Robert's main aim seems to be that of utilizing the deeper meaning of the given proverb to give his novel a serious political significance while protecting it from politically motivated censorship with the surface meaning. In this way the proverb reveals one more

---

[15] Stephen Arnold has written an interesting paper on this subject, "Popular Fiction in Tanzania: Its Background and Relation to East African Literature" in *When the Drum Beat Changes: Selected 1978 Annual ALA Papers* (Washington, D.C.: Three Continents Press, 1981). pp. 88-118.

way in which Shaaban Robert — whose penchant for allegory is often described — employs indirect methods to teach lessons.

Kusadikika is a story set in colonial Tanganyika disguised as a country floating somewhere in the sky. With this fantastic setting, Shaaban Robert managed so successfully to fool her royal majesty's representatives in the then Tanganyika Territory that they allowed the novel to be circulated in the country.

Kusadikika tells the story of a people who have been turned into robots. They believe whatever their rulers tell them. Several Kusadikikans visit other planets, and when they come back to Kusadikika with the knowledge that could help change people's lives, they are suppressed and jailed by the oppressive aristocratic government in Kusadikika. Karama ("Spiritual Talent") is one of the *Wajumbe* who have visited those other planets and who have witnessed so must development in those countries — development which he would like to see taking place in Kusadikika. He decides to lead his people's struggle by defending his case in court. His major opponent is the Prime Minister of Kusadikika — Majivuno ("Pride") who opposes everything that Karama says. Finally, however, Karama manages — through a long lecture in court — to convince the King about the truth behind the *Wajumbe's* demands. Consequently all the imprisoned *Wajumbe* — Buruhani ("A Gift of God"), Fadhili ("Mercy"), Kabuli ("Acceptance"), Auni ("Help"), Ridhaa ("Gracious Thanksgiving"), and Amini ("Trust") — are set free; and the development plans are carried out by the *Wajumbe*.

Now, let us examine the ways in which the quoted proverb builds this story. First, one must take into account the fact that *Kusadikika* belongs to the protest tradition in Swahili literature. It is, basically, about liberation struggle. Shaaban Robert lived and wrate at a time when contradtictions between colonial governments and the colonized people in Africa were rapidly sharpening. These struggles were not without leaders, and the leaders are represented in the novel by Karama and the other political detainees — the *Wajumbe*. They are the wounded cows. The proverb is double-edged. First, it constitutes an attempt to get the colonial government to grant a hearing to the people's case as a way of "licking their wounds." It is a plea to the colonial masters for leniency and consideration. This, of course, is an understandable shortcoming in Shabaan Robert's approach to the question. No colonial cow will ever lick the wounds of a colonized one. Always, in a colonial situation, the colonial cow plays the role of a hungry lion, and the colonized is turned into a hunted zebra.[16]

[16] Among the few works which have dealt with the writings of Shaaban Robert, two only seem to have noted this political fact. They are: Euphrase Kezilahabi's M.A. thesis, "Shaaban Robert: Mwandishi wa Riwaya" (Dar es Salaam, 1976; forthcoming in book form to be published by Tanzania Publishing House). This is the best work so far on Shaaban Robert's novels. It offers a very detailed and thought-provoking analysis of the novels. The second one is Don Bobb's article, "The Socio-Political Teachings and Art of Shaaban Robert's *Kufikirika* and *Kusadikika*" in *The Gar*, 32 (1978), pp. 28-30; short, swift and to the point.

For a predominantly German audience, a work which is probably worth reading concerning Shaaban Robert, is Rainer Arnold's Ph.D. dissertation "Untersuchungen zu Menschensbild und Gesellschaftskonzeption im Prosawerk Shaaban Robert' (Leipzig University, 1973).

T.S.Y. Sengo's "criticism" of *Kusadikika* in his *Shaaban Robert: Uhakiki wa Maandishi Yake* (Nairobi: Longman, 1975) is the shallowest work of the novel so far. Sengo chooses merely to paraphrase Shaaban Robert and Karama, sometimes adding his own dose of moralistic sermons. He ends the whole exercise by praising the "wisdom" and "hard-headedness" of the aristocracy for showing "clemency" to Karama and the other prisoners. The "critic" does not take us a single step towards an understanding of the socio-politico-economic forces operating in the novel.

The second significance of the proverb bears more weight in the novel. This is born out of the struggle that ensues in court between Karama and Majivuno, a conflict that symbolizes the struggle between the colonized people and the colonial power. In the context of this struggle, the proverb is intended as a call for other Kusadikikans, Karama's fellow colonised, to rise and help lick the wounds of those on the frontline of the libertaion struggle. It is a call for the people to join hands with those wounded in the war. Many critics who have overlooked the proverb in this novel have, in this way, missed a very significant clue to Shaaban Robert's clever dealing with the colonial situation. Within the proverb is concealed a sharp satire directed at the colonial regime in Tanganykia, a satire whose edge one might fail to see at first glance. This satirical aspect is also used as a tactic to counter the colonial government's censorship while at the same time conveying an important message to the people. This call for people to help each other, to lick each other's wounds, was essentially a bid for political mobilization. To miss this inner meaning of the proverb and its implications in *Kusadikika* is to miss the novel's battle cry.

The Herskovits tell us that a proverb is "a commentary on happenings that reveal the system of values under which (a) culture functions."[17] The culture revealed in the short story "Wali wa Ndevu" "Rice from the beards") is the feudal culture of slaves and slave masters. The former work for their master day in, day out, and in return they receive only left-overs, only the rice grains falling, contaminated from their masters' beards. And they are supposed to be grateful for such blessings.

In "Wali wa Ndevu," a story of how life used to be in old feudal Zanzibar is being narrated to senior government officials who are on an official visit to the Islands. The action occurs after many of them have repeatedly delivered their ready-made speeches, prepared for them by their principal Secretaries. Some officials, seemingly outraged, ironically clench their fists against the feudal lords in "Wali wa Ndevu;" some emotional ones issue battlecrys, disbelieving that such humiliation and degradation of man by man could really have existed. The story ends on a note of self-examination when the old man who is telling the story talks about some rumours which imply that even today, some people feed on others' rice-from-the-beard, that such humiliation and degradation still flourishes in these days of "independence." The immediate reaction of most of the honourable officials is "No!" To emphasize this revolutionary zeal, one of them — a university professor — starts singing *The Internationale*, the anthem of communism. It does not surprise the reader when the song fails to attract other singers among these honourable officials.

That, however, is not the end of the story. Among the visitors to the Isles, there is one young and daring journalist who feels compelled to write up the story in Mainland magazines and newspapers. But immediately after landing on the mainland soil, the journalist is given a stern warning, as are his fellow visitors to the Isles, not to mention anything about "the foolish old man's fictitious rice-from-the-beard story." This is, of course, a case of censorship. It is not desired

[17] Melville J. and Frances S. Herskovits, *Dahomean Narrative: A Cross-Cultural Analysis* (Evanston, Illinois, 1956), p. 56.

that the masses should hear the truth about life in neo-colonial societies and the way "independence" in some societies has stayed at the low level of mere beautiful flags and melodious anthems.

The satirical-political aspect in this short story is hidden in the half-finished pseudo-proverb, "Wali wa Ndevu." The story itself hints at this fact for it raises the question of who eats the rice-from-the-beard in the neo-colonies. The full version of this hinted-at pseudo-proverb could as well be "Wali wa Ndevu huliwa na Wanyonge" ("Rice from the beards is eaten by the oppressed").

The function of proverbs, especially the satirical-political ones, is basically to transmit evaluative messages to the listeners/readers; and their inner meanings usually hint at the causes and effects of situations in society and at suggestions for solutions. Among my students at the University of Dar es Salaam who had read "Wali wa Ndevu," the force of such hinting manifested itself in seminars and discussions. Often one would hear a student arguing that "Ili kuepukana na kulishwa wali wa ndevu, wakulima na wafanyakazi ulimwenguni hawana budi kufutilia mbali unyonge wao" ("So as not to feed on the rice-from-the-beards, peasants and workers of the world must get rid of their oppressors"). The essence of the pseudo-proverb in this short story, therefore, takes a higher plane as it issues forth a unversal call for the exploited people the world over to re-examine their conditions as oppressed masses and to find ways of stopping the humiliation of feeding on the rice from others' beards.

Conclusions

As more and more work is being done on Swahili and Tanzanian proverbs, it is imperative for genuine researchers and serious scholars to take into account the important fact of the dynamic nature of the proverbs. Many critics, scholars and authors seem to hold the view that the old contexts of *all* the proverbs remain the same today. They thus negate the potent behaviour of literature (both oral and written) which marches with changes and forces of time. This is, basically, the problem with Omolo's school of proverb-stories. Such stories are used to convey old moral prescriptions to cure complex social, political and economic diseases of today.

Shaaban Robert's *Kusadikika* and Tilumanya's "Wali wa Ndevu" on the other hand, have shown how the satirical-political perspectives of proverbs can be fully used to deliver important messages in proverb-stories. Also, and more important, I think, is the aspect of the transition from written to oral literature which is being born out of such stories. The imagery which readers get in the rice-from-the-beard episode, together with "Wali wa Ndevu's" simplicity of plot, make the message of the pseudo-proverb straightforward and very memorable. These factors create a very handy story, ready to be cited in many similar situations in the daily lives of the oppressed and exploited people. It is very easy to tell this story to the "illiterate" masses, and be able to touch some very sensitive points of their lives. In this way the dynamic nature of proverb-stories seems to be gaining new domains and dimensions. Scholars will no longer talk only about transition from oral to written literature but also about the osmotic pathway from written to oral literature. For committed proverb-stories, such phenomena will mean that litera-ture is drawn from the fountain of the people and returned to them not as the brackish poison in the *Hadithi za Kusisimua* series and similar works, but as the nourishment in *Kusadikika* and "Wali wa Ndevu."

BIBLIOGRAPHY

ARNOLD, Stephen. "Popular Fiction in Tanzania: Its Background and Relation to East African Literature." in C. Parker et al. eds. *When the Drum Beat Changes*. Washington D.C.: Three Continents Press, 1980, pp. 88-118.

BOBB, Don. "The Socio-Political Teachings and Art of Shaaban Robert's *Kufikirika* and *Kusadiki-ka*". *The Gar* 32 (1978), pp. 28-30.

DORSON, Richard M. *African Folklore*. Bloomington and London: Indiana University Press, 1972.

DUNDES, Alan. "On the Structure of the Proverb." *Proverbium* 25 (1975), pp. 961-973.

EASTMAN, Carol M. "The Proverb in Modern Written Swahili Literature: An Aid to Proverb Elicitation," in Richard M. Dorson, ed. *African Folklore*. Bloomington and London: Indiana University Press, 1972.

FINNEGAN, Ruch. *Oral Literature in Africa*. London: Oxford, 1971.

HARRIES, Lyndon. "African Proverbs: The Problem of Identification," in W.L. Ballard, ed.*Essays on African Literature*. Atlanta: School of Arts and Sciences, Georgia State University, 1973, pp. 39-96.

HERSKOVITS, Melville J. and Frances S. Herskovits. *Dahomean Narratives: A Cross Cultural Analysis*. Evanston, Illinois: Northwestern University Press, 1956.

HOLMAN. C.H. *A Handbook to Literature*. Indianapolis: Odyssey Press, 1975.

JASON, Heda. "Proverbs in Society: The Problem of Meaning and Function." *Proverbium* 17 (1971), pp. 617-623.

KEZILAHABI, E. "Riwaya za Kiswahili za Upelelezi," in *Kiswahili* 45(2) (1973), pp. 36-40.

—————— *Shaaban Robert: Mwandishi wa Riwaya*. Forthcoming. Dar es Salaam: Tanzania Pub-lishing House, 1981.

KIIMBILA, J.K. *Visa vya Walimwengu*. Dar es Salaam: Longmans, 1974.

KIRSCHENBLATT-BIMBLET, Barbara. "Toward a Theory of Proverb Meaning," in *Proverbium* 22 (1973), pp. 821-827.

KNAPPERT, Jan. "Rhyming Swahili Proverbs," and "Swahili Proverb Songs," in *African und Ubersee* 49 (1966), pp. 100-112, and 59 (1976), pp. 107-112 respectively.

LAIRD, Charlton. *Webster's New World Thesaurus.* New York: Popular Library, 1974.

MESSENGER, John C., Jr. "The Role of Proverbs in a Nigerian Judicial System" in *Southwestern Journal of Anthropology* 15 (1959), pp. 64-73. Reprinted in Alan Dundes, *The Study of Folklore*. Englewood Cliffs, N.J.: Prentice Hall, 1965, pp. 299-309.

MUHANDO, Penina and Ndyanao Balisidya. *Fasihi na Sanaa za Maonyesho*. Dar es Salaam: Tanzania Publishing House, 1976.

OMARI, C.K. et al. *Methali na Misemo Kutoka Tanzania*: 1 & 2. Nairobi: East African Literature Bureau, 1976 and 1978 respectively.

OMOLO, *Mtaka Yote Hukosa Yote*. Nairobi: Longman, 1968.

—————— *Mwerevu Hajinyoi*. Nairobi: Longman, 1971

—————— *Uhalifu Haulipi*. Nairobi: Longman, 1971.

OPOKU, Kofi Osare. *Speak to the Winds: Proverbs from Africa*, New York: Lithrop, Lee and Shepherd, 1975.

PARKER, Carolyn A. "Aspects of a Theory of Proverbs: Contexts and Messages of Proverbs in Swahili." PhD. Dissertation, University of Washington, 1974.

—————— "The Advice of Swahili Proverbs Concerning Money and Friendship." Mimeo in author's possession.

—————— "Techniques and Problems in Swahili Proverb Stories: The Case of Baalawy" in D. Dorsey et al. eds. *Design and Intent in African Literature*. Washington: Three Continents Press, 1982.

—————— and Douglas F. Kavugha. "Hadithi za Kusisimua: Crime and Passion in Swahili Literature," paper presented at the 1977 African Studies Association Meeting, Houston, November 1977, obtainable from the A.S.A.: University of California, Los Angeles.

ROBERT, Shaaban. *Kusadikika*. London: Thomas Nelson, 1951.

RUHUMBIKA, Gabriel, ed. *Parapanda*. Nairobi: East African Literature Bureau, 1976.

SENGO, T.S.Y. *Shabaan Robert: Uhakiki wa Maandishi Yake*. Dar es Salaam/Nairobi/Kampala: Longman, 1975.

SENKORO, F.E.M.K. "Remarks on Current Ideological Trends in the Swahili Novel," in *African Studies Association Archives 1978*. University of California, Los Angeles: A.S.A., 1978.

————— *Riwaya ya Kiswahili na Jamii*. Forthcoming. Dar es Salaam: Dar es Salaam University Press, 1981.

STEENSMA, Robert C. "A Legal Proverb in Defoe, Swift, and Shenstone," *Proverbium* 10 (1968), p. 248.

TAYLOR, Archer. "The study of Proverbs," *Proverbium* 1 (1965), pp. 1-10.

TAYLOR, W.E. *African Aphorisms, or Saws From Swahililand*. London: Sheldon Press, 1924. (First printed 1884).

TECHNIQUES AND PROBLEMS IN SWAHILI PROVERB STORIES: THE CASE OF BAALAWY

Carolyn A. Parker
University of Dar es Salaam

A two volume collection of short stories by Suleiman Oman Said Baalawy — *Hadithi za Bibi Maahira* (HBM: Grandmother Maahira's Stories) and *Bibi Maahira Tena* (BMT: Grandmother Maahira Again) — is written in the manner of a text familiar to the Swahili Coast, *A Thousand and One Nights*, that is, as a collection of unrelated stories told within a larger frame.[1] The frame provided by Baalawy is that of a grandmother, one Bibi Maahira, who wants to teach her two orphaned granchildren, Suud and Saida, proper values lest they be corrupted by their incorrigible neighbors. To do so, she sets out to tell them a series of stories which are based on and in illustration of twenty-eight traditional Swahili proverbs and one text — an inversion of the Golden Rule — which is said to be a common Swahili saying.[2]

The purposes of this paper are several. First, to describe the techniques by which Baalawy links the proverbs to their narratives. Second, to establish the problems which are associated with creating a proverb story. And, third, to show that, while the technique of using a proverb within such a narrative is less crucial than the degree and manner to which parallelism to the metaphor of the proverb text is reflected in the narrative, the technique of using a proverb may affect the understanding of the proverb itself.

Each of the stories in Baalawy's collection is presented in a regular pattern: first, the proverb text is given; second a literal explanation of the proverb is given along with what is intended to be an interpretation of the proverb's hidden, inner meaning and message and frequently emphasizes the grim consequences of failure to heed the message of the proverb, is told; and fourth, a song which refers to the story and/or the proverb is sung. At the beginning and end of each story the frame is maintained, although with varying detail throughout these narratives.

The stories themselves are in most cases original. One, the twelfth, is clearly a traditional oral narrative from the Swahili Coast which has been attested in the earliest collections of Swahili folklore.[3] Two or three others may have a traditional base, but this is not confirmed. None of the narratives is set in a large urban area, in contrast to much of modern Swahili writing. Most of the settings are rural or small

---

[1] *Hadithi za Bibi Maahira* (Nairobi: Evans Brothers, 1969); *Bibi Maahira Tena* (Nairobi: Evans Brothers, 1968). There is no clear reason why the second volume of the stories bears the earlier imprint date.

[2] Texts and translations of the proverbs are given in the Appendix. All translations of proverbs and quotes from Baalawy are my own.

[3] W.E. Taylor, *African Aphorism, or Saws from Swahili Land* (London: Sheldon Press, 1924 [first printed 1881]), pp. 91-92; C.G. Buttner, *Anthologie aus der Suaheli-Litteratur*, Vol. I (Berlin: Emil Felber, 1894), pp. 97-102, 125-130.

towns, mainly on Zanzibar and Pemba. Most of the stories are set in modern times; a few are set in a more or less remote past. Characters are frequently unnamed; almost all of them are male. Many of the stories tend to telescope many years of a character's lifetime into two or three pages, some even beginning before the main character is born.

Among the techniques available to Baalawy for linking the proverb text to the narrative which illustrates it are quotation, paraphrase, and allusion. The source for the proverbs may be a character in the narrative or the narrator, Bibi Maahira. Baalawy does not use all of these techniques and the proportions in which he does make use of them are varied. He makes mention of his tweny-nine texts thirty times, repeating six proverb texts a total of fourteen times. (See the Chart "Patterns of Proverb Use in Baalawy" that follows below.) About a third of the proverbs are spoken by a character in dialogue. No character paraphrases or alludes to a proverb. Slightly more than half of these proverbs are cited by the narrator either by quoting or by paraphrase. In some cases these paraphrases verge on allusion to the proverbs by the narrator, although they will be subsumed under the same category despite the fact that these categories are distinct by definition if not as evidenced by Baalawy. A fourth of the proverbs are omitted altogether from the narratives, being indiciated only by the title and introductory frame of the story. These patterns of proverb use are summarized in the following chart. The numbers indicate the number of the text in Baalawy's collection and correspond to the running numbers in the Appendix. The number of repetitions are indicated in parenthesis.

PATTERNS OF PROVERB USE IN BAALAWY

	Quoted by Character	Quoted by Narrator	Paraphrased by Narrator	Omitted	Repeated
PROVERB & NARRATIVE No.	1 3 7 8 12 18 (x3) 22 (x2) 24 27 28	2 3 4 6 10 11 18 19 23	5 6 10 13 17 20 26 27	9 14 15 16 21 25 29	3 (x2) 6 (x2) 10 (x2) 18 (x4) 22 (x2) 27 (x2)
TOTAL	10 (12)	9	8	7	6 (14)

In cases where the proverb is *spoken by the character*, the narratives come closest to representing an actual social context for proverb use. For example, in the twenty-second narrative, based on the proverb "The tongue has no bone," the character Sarenda is the strongest man in the village, winning all of the local wrestling matches. One day he single-handedly conquers sixteen thieves and boasts of it:

> Sarenda aliwaambia watu kuwa hapana anayeweza kupigana naye duniani. Wengine waliokuwa wajinga walikubali, na waliokuwa werevu kawakukubali bali walisema, 'Ulimi hauna mfupa' (BMT, p. 24).

> Sarenda told people that there was no one in the world who could fight with him (and win). Some who were fools agreed, and those who were clever didn't agree, rather they said, "The tongue has no bone."

Somewhat later when Sarenda arrogantly challenges some soldiers, they capture him through his own carelessness.

> Watu wa hapo kijijini waliposikia kuwa Sarenda ametiwa pingu na askari wawili dhaifu walistaajabu na kusema, "Aaa!! Ulimi hauna mfupa, ilikuwaje leo Sarenda kuwezekana?" (BMT, p. 25.).

> When the villagers heard that Sarenda had been shackled by two weak soldiers, they were amazed and said, "Aah!! The tongue has no bone, how was it that Sarenda was overcome?"

The ten narratives in which this pattern is followed demonstrate the typical pattern of roles in proverb use in social context: source, object, receiver, and audience. No matter whether any one of these narratives is appropriate as a proverb context, it is clear that veracity and realism are being sought in the use of proverbs in the narratives in this group.

In cases where the proverb is *quoted by the narrator*, the narrative comes closest to representing the stereotyped pattern of oral proverb stories. For example, the tenth story is based on the proverb "That which hits you is that which teaches you." A lazy, dirty youth is taught a lesson by the townspeople from whom he habitually mooches food. They refuse to feed him anymore and he must work if he is not to starve. He gets the message and eventually becomes a successful farmer. At the end of the story the narrator comments:

> Mtu huyo asingelipata raha hiyo lakini alipopigwa na njaa alifundishika, akaanza kufanya kazi na vitu vyake vilipokataliwa huko sokoni, vile vile, alifundishika akaacha tabia ya uchafu. Kwa hivyo ni kweli wanaposema watu kuwa ukupigao ndio ukufunzao (HBM, p. 36).

> That man would not have been so comfortable but when he was struck by hunger he was taught and he began to work. When his goods were refused in the marketplace, in the same way he was taught and he ceased being an unclean person. Therefore it is true what people say, that that which hits you is that which teaches you.

The nine narratives in which this pattern is followed come closest to the pattern or oral proverb narratives: a story illustrates the meaning (and sometimes the origin) of a proverb with the proverb text quoted at the end as a moral. The degree to which such narratives are more typical to African storytellers or to European collectors may be questioned, but these narratives do seem to indicate an adherence to an oral narrative pattern which promotes a moral and educational function for "proverb stories."

In cases where the proverb is *paraphrased by the narrator*, the use of proverbs becomes a blend of literary allusion, moralizing and, perhaps, belaboring the obvious. For example, the seventeenth narrative is based on the proverb, "Little by little fills the measure." At the end of the narrative the following analysis is given:

> Raha hiyo aliyoipata Musa ni kwa ajili ya ustahimilivu wake wa kudunduliza pesa na kutumia kwake kwa uangalifu, kwani aliweka pesa zake kidogo kidogo hata akawa tajiri, kama vile mtu anayetia mchele au mtama katika kibaba kidogo kidogo mpaka kikajaa (HMB, p. 76).

> The comfort which Musa got is due to his patience in saving money and his careful use of it, because he saved his money little by little until he became rich, just like someone who puts rice or millet in a pint measure little by little until it is full.

Less didactic and somewhat subtler is the following example, from the twenty-seventh story, based on the proverb, "After distress (comes) relief." Bibi Maahira alludes to the proverb and uses this allusion to signal a turning point in the plot:

> Basi hapo ndipo ilipomalizika dhiki ya Saburi na ndipo alipoanza faraji yake (BMT, p. 64).

> Well this was when Saburi's distress ended and when his relief began.

Although the didacticism and paraphrase of the former is more characteristic of this type of proverb usage in this collection, the allusion and structural significance of the latter, as heavy handed as it is, comes closer to what would be termed literary use of proverbs rather than functional use in social context.

Interestingly enough, those narratives in which *no mention of the proverb* is made, aside from the introductory discourse on its literal and inner meanings, involve the most complicated and obscure proverbs in the entire corpus. And where the proverbs are rather more overt in their meanings, the stories seem to obscure the meaning rather than clarify it. The fifteenth story, based on "Fools are the ones who are eaten," is a case in point.

Baalawy explains the proverb through Bibi Maahira as follows:

> ...maana ya fumbo hili ni kuwa watu ambao ni wajinga huliwa, yaani huliwa na wale ambao ni waerevu. Undani wa fumbo hili ni kuwa mjinga hajui jema wala baya, anaweza kuelekezwa njia ambayo ni mbaya kwake na akaifuata. Kwa hivyo mtu wa namna hiyo akipambana na yule ambaye ni mwerevu, huliwa yaani anaweza kumwambia uongo na akamnyang'anya kama alicho nacho (HBM, p. 60).

> ...the meaning of this proverb is that people who are fools are always eaten, that is, they are eaten by those who are clever. The inner meaning of this proverb is that a fool does not know good or bad and he may be led

to a path which is bad for him and follow it. Therefore if a person of this sort meets one who is clever, he is eaten, that is he can lie to him and rob him if he has anything.

Interviews with informants from the Kenya Coast in 1972 and 1979 confirm that the proverb is a statement of fact: ignorant people get taken in.[4] The common interpretation of the term *mjinga* is one who is foolish by virtue of ignorance and inexperience, not necessarily by virtue of innate stupidity or lack of intelligence. Informants disagree, however, with Baalawy and his narrator regarding the inner meaning of the proverb and its use. Indeed, what Baalawy labels as inner meaning is merely a restatement of the literal meaning; Baalawy does not, in fact, provide an interpretation of the proverb's inner meaning, nor does he indicate how the proverb would be applied in context.

Informants suggest that the proverb is a slur on character since ignorance is inexcusable when there are those around who can give (or could have given) advice and information. The message of the proverb is that one must, in any case, always be aware of the situation in which he finds himself, to see that he is not cheated or misused. The proverb may be used as a subtle warning to someone that he is being fooled, as well as to criticize someone for remaining ignorant when knowledge is there for the asking. While there is not criticism in the proverb of those who would deceive a fool, the deceiver may use the proverb of himself or be told the proverb in bragging about or praising a successful deception.

This proverb clusters with serveral other Swahili proverbs, which suggest similar messages:

> KUULIZA SI UJINGA, to ask is not foolishness.
> ASIYEULIZA HANA LA KUJIFUNZA, S/he who does not ask has nothing to learn.
> MWENYE MACHO HAAMBIWI, "TAZAMA!" One with eyes is not told, "Look!"
> DALILI YA MVUA NI MAWINGU, The sign of rain is clouds.

All refer to the necessity to be aware of what goes on around oneself and to eschew ignorance.

The narrative, which accompanies this proverb in Baalawy's collection, is summarized as follows:

> There was a poor man who was too lazy to work. he bought a book for a shilling and became a magician-diviner. He used a board and white sand from the beach for divining and various roots which he had dug up for curing.
>
> This charlatan went to a village and through practical knowledge and common sense divined the troubles of several people, including a man who suspected his brother of enmity and a woman who suffered the usual difficulties of pregnancy. Both felt cured by the roots, which he sold to them at exorbitant cost.
>
> In the town there was a Sultan, Masuna, who had six captive lions and

---

[4] Mahir Said (6/72) and Mohammed Maulana (9/72), both from Mombasa, then living in Lamu. Sauda Said (3/79), also from Mombasa, interviewed in Austin, Texas.

who was at war with and often defeated by another Sultan, Sabahun. Fearing defeat, Masuna went to the charlatan to be advised. His troubles, which were well-known in the town, were "divined." The Sultan paid 2000 sh. to her the advice of the charlatan's "genie."

With much warning and drama, the charlatan says the message of the genie will be written on a paper held over a smoking fire by the Sultan. The charlatan went into a trance, and when he collapsed, the Sultan removed the paper from the smoke. On it was written in red the advice to set a trap for Sabahun's soldiers with the six lions at the river.

The trap was set and the attacking soldiers annihilated. A counter-attack against Sabahun was successful and the charlatan is made prime minister.

The genie's writing was accomplished with lime juice, which is invisible until the paper is smoked.

The question that arises from this illustration of the proverb is: exactly how are the fools eaten? Or, more abstractly, how does the narrative parallel the metaphor of the proverb? How does it evidence proper application of this particular proverb to this particular context? At which point in the narrative do we find clear need and illustration of the proverb's message?

All of the charlatan's clients do indeed pay a high price for his perception and common sense, but in all cases the help they are given seems to be worth the price, for all parties benefit from the interaction. The possibility that they might them-selves have shown common sense, or at least sought *free* advice, may show them to be fools who have been eaten. Or, perhaps the trick with lime juice should have been seen for what it was.[5] Indeed, the Sultan may be viewed from a contemporary perspective as just a bit gullible with his belief in genies. However, my data indicate that this story does not provide an adequate parallel to the metaphor of the proverb, i.e., the fools are not sufficiently foolish (they live in a time and place whre divination and supernatural beings fit with their cosmology) nor are the fools sufficiently eaten (they are, after all, satisfied with the diviner's diagnosis and the Sultan does win his war). Baalawy, on the other hand, does not provide enough information in his interpretation of the proverb to answer this question for us.

Baalawy's narrator often tends to elaborate on and analyze a proverb's applica-tion to her stories; for this story, however, the frame only indicates that her grandson tests the trick with lime juice, and even the usual perfunctory note that the children went to bed after her song is not given. No comment, then, within the story in the frame suggests that the message of the proverb is awareness and caution, or that this message should be heeded. In fact, the rewards given the charlatan and the adjectives used to describe him seem to praise him and his industrious trickery, while de-emphasizing any criticism of the ignorant people he tricked.

The analysis of this proverb and its story suggests that there are two fun-

---

[5] It might be noted that this same technique was offered for sale to me at the price of 100 sh. (about US $14) in Lamu in 1972, the technique to be revealed after I had paid the price. Fortunately, I had no need to write secret messages and could not, in any case, spare the cash, so that I was neither "eaten" nor allowed to display my ignorance, inexperience, or gullibility.

damental problems confronting the writer of a proverb story. These problems parallel the problems which must be faced by the proverb user in social interaction. First, there is the matter of shared knowledge of the proverb in terms of its literal meaning, inner meaning, and accepted patterns of use in social context. Second, there is the matter of creating a narrative which parallels the metaphor of the proverb and highlights its message, i.e., a narrative which provides a suitable context for the proverb.

No matter whether one technique or another for citing or omitting a proverb is adopted, and disregarding whether Baalawy's interpretation of a given proverb agrees with data from any other source, there still remain all of the difficulties of the second problem — parallelism and message. To be parallel, the narrative must not be a literal re-enactment of the proverb text, as for example is the first narrative, based on "he who does not heed the advice of an elder breaks a leg," in which a young man doesn't listen to his grandfather and winds up in the hospital with a broken leg. Literalness is a factor negatively valued in both Western and swahili standards for proverb use. Literalness seems, however, to be a tendency in this collection.[6]

To be parallel, the narrative must also demonstrate the cause and effect relationship of the proverb text, as well as that of the underlying message. The cause and effect relationship of the underlying message is the relationship between the circumstances which suggest that a particular proverb is both appropriate and necessary and the use of the proverb at the right moment in the situation to communicate the desired message.

The inner meaning or message of the proverb, particularly as it is revealed by use in social context, is often contradictory to or hidden in the literal meaning, e.g., "Fools are the ones who are eaten," but people should try not to be fools; "One who does good does good for himself," but one should understand that failure to do good will lead to bad consequences[7]; "One who climbs a ladder always comes down," so he should be nice to the people below him while he is at the top.[8]

The cause and effect of the literal proverb statement is, more often than not, exaggerated in these narratives. This is both unrealistic and negatively valued in Western standards for the literary use of proverbs, although it is not clear whether such exaggeration may be negatively valued in Swahili letters. Exaggeration does seem to be characteristic of much of contemporary Swahili popular writing, as well as some of the traditional epic poetry. On the other hand, it is subtlely which is valued in proverb texts and contexts. It remains to be seen whether subtlety is a valued aspect of the proverb story.

---

[6] The tendency toward literalness in this collection has already been pointed out in Carolyn A. Parker, "The Advice of Elders, a Broken Leg, and a Swahili Proverb Story," in *Artist and Audience: African Literature as a Shared Experience*, edited by Richard O. Priebe and Thomas A Hale (Washington, D.C.: Three Continents Press, 1979), pp. 49-59.

[7] MTENDA VYEMA HUTENDEA NAFSI YAKE, discussed in Carolyn A. Parker, "Social Balance and the Threat of Revenge: The Message of Some Swahili Proverbs," *Greenfield Review*, 8, 1-2 (Spring 1980), 163-175.

[8] *Hadithi za Bibi Maahira*, pp. 5-7.

In contrast, however, to this exaggeration of the literal statement and parallel elements, the message of the proverb is sometimes obscured by the narrative itself. The stories of the collection get progressively longer as Baalawy warms to his task. They suggest themes and values unrelated to the proverb and their values, such as western education, modernization, acquisition of wealth, the rightful dominance of the government. The proverbs, on the other hand, are oriented toward family relationships, patience and hard work, the consequences of wrong-doing, and the value of experience.[9]

The successful revelation of a proverb's message would seem logically to have little to do with the technique for incorporating a proverb into a narrative. At first glance it would seem that it makes little difference whether a character or the narrator quotes the proverb, whether it is given in full, paraphrased or omitted altogether. But the contrary may be the case. Proverbs are normally used purpo-sively, and the purpose is normally to communicate a message. The message is undoubtedly clearest when the narrator paraphrases the proverb as she explains it; there is no ambiguity here nor is there much aesthetic pleasure in Bibi Maahira's case. The message is most ambiguous when the proverb is omitted from the narrative, if for no other reason than that many proverbs can be used to communi-cate several different messages, e.g., criticism, approval, justification, and warn-ing. In Baalawy's case, at least, quotation of the proverb removes some of the ambiguity about the type of message being communicated and allows for some enjoyment of the application of the proverb to the narrative situation. Although these stories are clearly didactic, an intention expressed repeatedly in the frame, there is greater appeal in those narratives where realism in proverb use is attemp-ted, i.e., when a character speaks the proverb in context, for the didactic element is less overt.

The techniques for using a proverb in narrative and the problems associated with creating a suitable narrative for a proverb are not unrelated, especially when the declared goal is interpretation of the meaning of a proverb. Once there is a shared understanding of the proverb's literal and inner meanings, the story must reflect these by parallel. The message of the proverb is revealed in literature, as it is in social interaction, by its use in context. The technique for using a proverb in such a narrative is an integral factor in the success or failure of a proverb story, for when a clear message is intended, the message must be clearly given.

APPENDIX

1. ASIYESIKIA LA MKUU HUVUNJIKA MGUU.
    s/he who does not hear /it of/ superior person /is always broken/ leg
    One who fails to heed the advice of an elder breaks a leg.
2. MPANDA NGAZI HUSHUKA.
    one who climbs /ladder, staircase/ always descends
    One who climbs the stairs usually descends.
3. MTAKA CHA MVUNGUNI SHARTI AINAME.
    one who wants /it of/ underneath (the bed) /necessity/ s/he is to stoop
    One who wants what is under the bed must stoop.

---

[9] In regard to the latter theme, see Carolyn A. Parker, "Swahili Proverbs: The Nature and Value of Painful Experience," *GAR*, 32 (1978), 23-24, 26.

4. MTI HUULIWA NA MATUNDA YAKE.
tree /always killed/ by /fruits/ its
   A tree is killed by its fruit.
5. BORA KUJIKWAA KIDOLE KULIKO KUJIKWAA ULIMI.
better /to stumble, trip oneself/ toe /where there is/ to stumble, trip oneself /tongue
   Better to stumble with the toe than with the tongue.
6. MAJI YAKIMWAGIKA HAYAZOLEKI.
water /if it is spilled/ it is not swept up
   Spilled water cannot be swept up.
7. BAA HALIMPATI MMOJA.
disaster /it does not get him/ one person
   Disaster doesn't come to just one person.
8. UDONGO UPATIZE ULIMAJI.
clay /get it/ it is wet
   Mold clay while it is wet.
9. MTENDA VYEMA HUTENDEA NAFSI YAKE.
one who does /good things/ always does to /self/ his
   One who does good does it to himself.
10. UKUPIGAO NDIO UKUFUNZAO.
that which hits you /it is indeed/ that which teaches you
   That which hits you is that which teaches you.
11. MUANGAZA MBILI MOJA HUMPONA.
one who fixes attention on /two/ one /always escapes him
   One who concentrates on two (things), one always escapes him.
12. MCHIMBA KISIMA HUINGIA MWENYEWE.
one who digs /a well/ always enters /himself
   One who digs a well (for others) enters it himself.
13. SIMBA MWENDA KIMYA NDIYE MLA NYAMA.
lion /one who goes/ quietly /he is indeed/ one who eats /meat
   The lion who goes quietly is the one who eats meat.
14. VITA VYA PANZI NI NEEMA YA KUNGURU.
battle /it of/ grasshoppers /it is/ bountiful harvest /it of/ pied crow
   The battle of grasshoppers is the harvest of the crow.
15. WAJINGA NDIO WALIWAO.
fools /they are indeed/ they who are eaten
   Fools are the ones who are eaten.
16. MFA MAJI HUSHIKA MAJI.
one who dies /water/ always grasps /water
   A drowning man grasps water.
17. HABA NA HABA HUJAZA KIBABA.
little /and/ little /always fills/ pint measure
   Little by little fills the measure
18. AJALI HAIKIMBILIKI.
fate /it cannot be run from
   Fate cannot be escaped.
19. KUKULACHO KIMO NGUONI MWAKO.
it which eats, bites you /it is inside/ in clothes /in yours
   That which bites you is in your clothes.
20. MALI YA BAHILI HULIWA NA WADUDU.
wealth, property /it of/ miser /always eaten/ by /insects
   The property of a miser is eaten by insects.
21. MKAMIA MAJI HAYANYWI.
one who insistently demands, extorts /water/ s/he does not drink it
   One who demands water does not drink it.
22. ULIMI HAUNA MFUPA.
tongue /it does not have/ bone
   The tongue has no bone.
23. MCHAMA AGO HANYELE.
one who moves from /fishing camp/ he does not defecate in
   One who will return to a fishing camp does not defecate there.

24. UKIONA VINAELEA VIMEUNDWA.
   if you see /they are floating/ they have been created, built
   > If you see (vessels) floating, they have been built (by someone's labor).

25. MSTAHAMILIVU HULA MBIVU.
   one who is patient /always eats/ ripe, cooked
   > A patient man eats ripe (fruit).

26. TAMAA MBELE MAUTI MYUMA.
   desire /in front/ death /behind
   > Desire is in front, death is behind.

27. BAADA YA DHIKI FARAJI.
   after /it of/ distress /relief
   > After distress (comes) relief.

28. MCHAGUA JEMBE SI MKULIMA.
   one who chooses /hoe/ he is not /farmer
   > One who is choosey about a hoe is not a farmer.

29. USIMFANYE MTU JAMBO USILOPENDA KUFANYIWA.
   don't do to him /person/ matter /it which you do not like/ to be done to
   > Don't do something to someone which you would not like to have done to yourself.

THE WEST

THE ABSENCE OF THE PASSIONATE LOVE THEME IN AFRICAN LITERATURE

Phanuel Akubueze Egejuru
Imo State University, Etiti Campus

In the context of this paper, love strictly refers to passionate love as opposed to deep devotion to and affection for a person. In passionate love, the one in love is literally possessed of the sentiment, and wishes to consume or be consumed by the loved one. A person possessed of this kind of love is literally sick with love and cannot be cured until — in Gidean terms — he conquers or possesses the loved one. But even when this apparent conquest is made, the fever of love continues to burn.

This kind of love theme abounds in western literature, but to date, passionate love as a major theme is absent from African literature. Although European literature from the Middle Ages to the nineteenth century is saturated with the theme of passionate love, there is nothing so far in African literature to parallel love stories like, for instance, Tristan and Iseult, or Abelard and Heloise; nor do we have anything to liken to Romeo and Juliet, Manon Lescaut, Madame Bovary, and a host of other passionate love figures of European literature.

The point here is not to say that passionate love does not exist among Africans, but that it has not yet formed a major focus in any African literary work. Indeed, fragments of passionate love appear here and there as side plots, digressions and so forth, to enhance main themes which often have nothing to do with passionate love. The preponderance of this theme in western literature can be explained by the norms and values of the west. Here love is an ultimate value. It is an achievement to make love to the loved one, because it is a way of proving one's virility as well as one's acceptability to the loved one. Being able to love in this way is both self-gratifying as well as self-fulfilling for the lover.

Here is one true-to-life example of what self-fulfillment through love can mean to a western man. Edward VIII of England set an unprecedented example of heroic dramatization of a man's personal self-realization through love. He abdicated the British throne in order to marry a catholic, thrice divorced American woman, with whom he lived in exile for more than thirty years. To Edward VIII, the fulfillment of himself as a man was far more important and attractive than the pomp and pageantry of British monarchy. Love is seen here as very fundamental to the western concept of self-fulfillment, and it is basic to intimate personal relationships.

To an African, it is unthinkable for a man to abandon his ancestral home in pursuit of a woman in the name of love. To him, expressions like "I can't live without you," "I love you more than anything else in the world," are purely nonsensical romantic jargon which only expose the apparent lover to ridicule in the eyes of the peers. In fact, to emphasize the foolishness of "dying" for love, there is a simple riddle in Igbo which asks the question: "If your mother and your wife are drowning, whom would save?" To every Igbo man, the answer is "my mother," for he knows that he can only have one mother, but can marry as many wives as he can afford.

In Africa, the ultimate value is not self-fulfillment in the act of loving; it is rather the ability to create life through the act of loving. Every African community prides itself on the number of people it has. Every member of the community strives to contribute to the community's human resources by producing as many children as one possibly can. Any person who is unable to make this contribution either through his or nature's fault, is subject to public pity, humiliation or derision. Unlike in the west, making love for the African is only a means to the greater end of acceptance by and integration into one's community by creating life. To the African, the worst that could happen to a person is the inability to procreate.

That love making is only a means is further illustrated in various practices such as parental arrangement of marriage for the children. This practice often eliminates the idea of falling in love before marriage because, most often the would-be couple have never met each other. They only hope to like each other enough to marry. In Feraoun's *Les Chemins qui montent* for instance, the hero Mokrane must be content to settle with Ouiza as has been arranged by their parents. It is only after the final marriage rituals have been performed that Mokrane "must start thinking honorably about his wife and falling discreetly in love with her."[1] Thus, even when one is married, one must be discreet in showing one's love because it is not a virtue to parade one's passionate yearnings for a beloved. If a man is found too yielding to his wife's demands in the name of love, such a man is henpecked in the eyes of his peers. The same caution is required of a woman, or else other women would gossip about her uncontrollable sexual drive. The extent to which open avowal of love is frowned upon and therefore kept in check, could be seen in the fact that the expression "I love you" is almost never used in many African languages. Thus we often hear: "He loves her," "she loves him," but the two in love hardly confront each other and say "I love you."

Speaking about the discretion with which the Algerian society treats love, Mohammed Dib said: "L'amour (le sentiment, l'act et le mot) est considéré comme une chose indécente et malhonête"[2] [love (the sentiment, the act and the word) is considered an indecent and dishonest thing]. Again in an interview Dib comments on the ignorance of Algerian women in matters of love: "Le mot lui-même 'amour' est encore inconnu dans son acceptation véritable de beaucoup de femmes"[3] [the word itself 'love' is still unknown in its truest sense by many women]. Dib's observation is equally true of many women in other parts of Africa.

To further prove that passionate love is very secondary in life-long relationships between men and women in Africa, the idea of sexual incompatibility is non-existent. It is strongly frowned upon if a girl has premarital sex with the would-be husband or any other man before her marriage, because the breaking of her virginity is to be publicly celebrated and rewarded. The couple is mainly interested in having children and not in having sex purely for its own sake and enjoyment. They therefore begin making love after marriage in order to have

[1] Mouloud Feraoun, *Les Chemins qui montent* (Paris: Seuil, 1957)
[2] Mohammed Dib in a letter cited by Aida Bamieh in her thesis: "The Development of the Novel and Short Story in Modern Algerian Literature" (London School of Oriental and African Studies, 1971), p. 300.
[3] Mohammed Dib, Interview with *L'Afrique Littéraire et Artistique*, no. 18 août, 1971.

children. To further illustrate the overriding importance of procreation, the Yoruba people have a custom whereby the would-be bride undergoes a testing period during which she is expected to get pregnant. If she fails to get pregnant within the given period, the marriage arrangements may be called off.

Procreation more than anything else accounts for the practice of polygyny in Africa. Since a man aims at having as many children as he possibly can, and since a woman's childbearing age is limited, the man is free to marry other wives to help him in his childbreeding process. The women themselves accept as a matter of course that the purpose of marriage is to have children. And most of them demonstrate this by stopping sexual intercourse when they pass childbearing age. This behaviour is well illustrated in Grace Ogot's short story "Tekayo," where we find Lakech who "had passed the age of childbearing and no longer went to Tekayo's hut at night, she was his wife and he loved her."[4] Here the love which has grown out of marriage remains strong without seeking proof of its existence or affirmation in lovemaking.

One may conclude thus far that the norms and values of the African people account for the authors' silence on passionate love as a major theme in literature. However, this does not mean that the sentiment and concept are lacking in the culture. The point is that Africans conceive of love differently, and they have a very different way of approaching the subject. Indeed, live is very much a part of living, but the expressions of it are more complex than a non-African would care to analyze. The kind of love which dominates in Africa is deep devotion which is not necessarily oriented towards consummation in sexual act, nor is it necessarily between two people of opposite sexes. It is the kind that gives birth to a blood pact between two people of the same or opposite sexes, to remain loyal to the vows they made to each other.

There are numerous examples of deep devotion in African literature, especially in the works set in the village. We find it mostly among husbands and wives where the emotional commitment can reach a point where a couple literally cannot live without each other. In Flora Nwapa's *Idu* we find the love between Idue and Adiewere, her husband. Their love for each other was so much and so obvious that the second wife couldn't stand it and had to run away. When Adiewere died suddenly, it took only twenty-eight days before Idu joined him in the land of the dead.[5]

In *Things Fall Apart*, Ozoemena, the oldest wife of Ndulue, dies a few hours after she learns of her husband's death. To rationalize her death Obierika recalls: "It was always said that Ndulue and Ozoemena had one mind. I remember when I was a young boy there was a song about them. He could not do anything without telling her."[6] In a way, Ndulue betrays the spiritual vow he made to Ozoemena by dying without telling her, but she would not be left behind.

Doguicimi, the heroine of Paul Hazoume's novel *Doguicimi*, underwent torture, imprisonment and death in the name of conjugal fidelity to her dead husband.

---

[4] Grace Ogot, "Tekayo" in *African Writing Today*, ed. Ezekiel Mphahlele (London: Penguin Books, 1974), p. 114.
[5] Flora Nwapa, *Idu* (London: Heinemann, 1970), p. 218.
[6] Chinua Achebe, *Things Fall Apart* (Greenwich, Connecticut: Fawcett Publications, 1959), p. 65-66.

She, of her own free will, walked into the vault and ordered the people to roll the stone over the entrance.

In Nazi Boni's *Crépuscule des temps anciens*, we find a kind of idyllic love between Terhé and Hankki. They cannot marry because they are too closely related. They make a blood pact to remain inseparable even by death. After Terhé's death, Hankki went every day to lie on his grave and pray for death, for custom forbids suicide. After a few weeks she succeeds in joining her beloved in the land of the spirits.

In all these instances, love is not the main theme. At best it could be a side plot as in *Crépuscule des temps anciens* or a digression as in *Things Fall Apart*. More often than not, love is used to illuminate the main theme as in *Doguicimi* and *Idu*. In *Doguicimi* for instance, the author's intention was to present the overbearing ceremonies and rituals of Ghezo's Dahomey in the 19th century. The interest in the heroine is less in her undying love and fidelity to a dead husband than in her portrayal of ideals of courage, stoicism and patriotism. The death of these women after their beloved ones would not be seen by many Africans as gestures of love. Africans would more likely view their death as part of the mysteries of the Arican universe. The Igbo people would see it as a bargain which the couples struck with their Chi before ever they were created.

In contrast to the village novels, the city-set novels have characters whose concept of love has become more western because of their western education. We find fragments of passionate love acted out by these westernized Africans. Their show of love is a farce because they rarely have the nerve to play out their parts. There is always the society's traditional value looming in the background. And more often than not they give up their fantasy in deference to tradition.

A classical example of love which gave way to tradition is that of Obi and Clara in Achebe's *No Longer at Ease*. Both Obi and Clara studied in England. There they fell in love and continued to be in love after their return to Nigeria. Clara got pregnant and Obi is willing to marry her. But they have to consult their parents before finalizing the marriage arrangements. Obi's relatives make the necessary inquiries in which it is revealed that Clara is an *osu*. Obi cannot marry her, and in spite of his westernization he cannot fight this custom. However, Obi has the choice to defy tradition and join the ranks of the *osu* by marrying one of them, but his mother threatens suicide should he go through with such a marriage. Clara is forced to have an abortion and Obi pays the expenses and their love story ends. This story is only a side plot to enhance the major theme of a man's struggle to reconcile his personal ideals and "the ways of the people."

In Kateb Yacine's novel *Nedjma*, the heroine Nedjma is courted by four men, each of whom knows he can never get her because her mother has already made a choice for her. With a heavy heart, Nedjma marries her mother's choice. The author comments on this customary matchmaking by parents: "Kamel s'est marié parce que sa mère l'a voulu, Nedjma s'est mariée parce que sa mère l'a exigé"[7] (Kamel is married because his mother wanted it, Nedjma is married because her mother insisted on it).

Commenting on the constant failure of lovers to consummate their love,

[7] Kateb Yacine, *Nedjma* (Paris: Seuil, 1956), p. 67.

Charles Bonn says:

> Dès la littérature classique algérienne, une sorte de fatalité semble donc peser déjà sur le sentiment amoureux. L'amour est toujours impossible. Bien plus rare sont les personnages qui y croient et s'ils le font ils s'en avisent toujours trop tard.[8]
>
> [Starting from the classical Algerian literature, a sort of destiny thus seems to hang over the sentiment of love. Love is always impossible. More rare are characters who believe in it, and if they do, they always realize it too late] (Translation mine).

Bonn's observation is quite true. Not only is romantic love impossible, very few Africans truly believe in it, and those who claim to believe, always give it up due to family and societal pressures.

In Peter Abrahams' *Path of Thunder*, Lanny, a black man falls in love with Sadie, an Afrikaner girl. Both of them hoped to set a record for interracial marriage. In the end both lovers are murdered and their ambition to break a long-standing taboo is foiled. Similar to Abrahams' Lanny is Ekwensi Bayo in *People of the City*. Bayo loves a Lebanese girl whom he visits secretly against the girl's brother's warnings. Their love suddenly ends when Zamil, the girl's brother, shoots and kills Bayo to prevent him from marrying his sister.

Again, in "Night of Freedom," by Ekwensi, we find a more penetrating probe into interracial love as well as a probe into one's freedom to love whomsoever one desires. Chini is a Nigerian girl educated in England. She has returned and is working as a secretary. She falls in love with a Frenchman and often she debates within herself: "I don't love this man...I love him...But he is French. It doesn't matter...it does." Suddenly she seems to have found the answer and she proudly declares:

> Nigeria independent was not Nigeria colonial. Women today were in a different position. Black and white, yellow or red, when love whispered, it was the same response. But WHY fall in love with a Frenchman?[9]

One sees in Ekwensi's story that the heroine is not really convinced that she should love a "stranger," besides, she wasn't sure that her dear François would be willing to love in the Nigerian way, as she would soon explain. François says to her: "Nigerian girls do not know the meaning of love." Chini asks him to explain it to her and he says: "It's not easy to explain. You see, love is all-consuming, a personal affair between two people." Chini quickly retorts: "That's in Europe. In Africa it is a *public* affair. Everyone is concerned. My mother is concerned, so are my mother's people. My father is dead but my uncle and his family must know. I did not drop from the sky you know."[10] While they were taking a walk in the city, François tried to kiss Chini in public, and Chini who had just declared love a public affair, recoils from François saying: "But François we're in public!" Love between two people in Africa is a public affair because the two must be aiming at their society's cherished value of procreation. And this must be properly accomplished through marriage which binds not only the couple but their families,

---

[8] Charles Bonn, *La Littérature Algérienne de la langue française* (Ottawa: Naaman, 1974), p. 134.
[9] Cyprian Ekwensi, "Night of Freedom" in *African Writing Today*, ed. E. Mphahlele (London: Penguin Books, 1974), p. 26.
[10] Ibid.

villages, towns or even countries!

One could go on and on to cite examples of abortive passion-oriented love among Africans. But it would be fair to mention that a few of them do marry even for a short period of time, and still very few marry and live happily ever after. Among the few whose marriages lasted for a short while are Ahouna's in Quénum's *Un Piège sans fin* and Medza's in Mongo Beti's *Mission terminée*. Ahouna woos and captures the sensitive soul of a young virgin with his music. They marry, and shortly after, his wife starts to see visions of another woman in her husband's eyes. Her imagination runs away with her and Ahouna, who nearly goes insane for this senseless accusation, runs away from home. His flight leads to a chain of tragic events — manslaughter, imprisonment, torture and finally public execution by burning. As in many other African novels, the love which triggered off the chain of tragic events in Ahouna's life only served as a mere digression. The author's intention is to illustrate a Sartrean existentialist philosophy of man trapped in a world of endless snares.

In *Mission terminée*, Medza is initiated into love and sex. He is finally tricked into marrying the girl who broke his virginity. Soon after his return home, his excitement about love and marriage burn out. With his semi-French education, he could not take all that it required to integrate fully into his community. He deserts his young wife and runs off to the city for more exciting and dangerous living. He actually rejects love and salvation which the village offered and heads for an obvious self-annihilation in the metropolis.

Among very few westernized Africans who marry and supposedly live happily ever after, are Odili and Edna in Achebe's *A Man of the People* and Sago and Beatrice the second in Ekwensi's *People of the City*. However, Odili owes the realization of this marriage to the coup d'état which toppled Nanga's government, because if the coup had not taken place, there is no reason to believe that Edna would have given up the rich and influential, albeit corrupt Nanga for the poor and powerless school teacher.

Sago and Beatrice the second get married after much opposition from the bride's father. The young couple had to emigrate to the Gold Coast to start a new life. It is not explained why it was so necessary for them to leave their country. Could it be possible that family and social pressures would have prevailed against their love?

How then does one explain the failure of western oriented love among westernized Africans? Is it not possible that these love affairs failed because those involved were not being true to themselves, that deep down, they desired and preferred to achieve a balance between their aspirations and the expectations of their societies? It would be no exaggeration to say that very few, if any, Africans are capable of making love their ultimate value.

In addition to the reasons and examples given so far for the absence of the passionate love theme in African literature, several African writers have some other plausible reasons and explanations. Many of the writers correctly say that African literature goes in phases. Thus, the early writings started with re-evaluation and restoration of African traditional values, and the declaration of these values to the west which had long despised them out of conceit, and for their own politico-economic purposes. Next came the phase for protests and attacks on colonialism. And presently they are dealing with socio-political situations of independent Africa. After this phase they may move to more 'universal' themes.

When asked why there is no love theme in African literature, Ezekiel Mphahlele said: "I think it is because we started writing as a result of depressing conditions....I think we will settle down to certain universal issues as we go along."[11] Speaking on the same subject, Mohammed Dib said:

> Dans les conditions telles qu'elles ont été décrites par Feraoun, par Mouloud Mammeri, par moi-même, il était impensable de pouvoir écrire un roman d'amour. Il était impensable de parler d'un tel sentiment.[12]
> [Under the circumstances such as described by Feraoun, by Mouloud Mammeri, and by myself, it was unthinkable to be able to write a novel of love. It was unthinkable to talk of such a sentiment] (translation mine).

Unlike many other writers, Ngugi wa Thiong'o does not believe in universalism. Ngugi asks:

> What is a greater theme than the struggle of a people to liberate themselves? In fact this is a struggle in essence to liberate man. Ours is not a literature moving away from man, not a man contemplating his state of helplessness in this world. As far as this struggle for liberation continues, we cannot say that we have exhausted the topic (of Africa), to say so amounts to saying that African people have ceased to exist.[13]

This view of Ngugi's goes a long way toward explaining why he presents the love sick Karanga as a very weak and pathetic figure in *A Grain of Wheat*. Karanja is despised by his peers because he is foolishly and hopelessly in love with the married Mumbi. Because of his love for her, he does not take any active part in the "Emergency." In this way Karanja lets his love for a woman interfere with fulfilling his patriotic duties for the cause of Independence. In his *Critical Evaluation of African Literature*, Edgar Wright refers to Karanja in these terms: "If there is a non-heroic all-for-love theme, Karanja embodies it and thereby gains for himself the contempt if not the hatred of all who suffered for the cause of Independence."[14] As far as Ngugi and several other African writers are concerned, it is foolish or unthinkable to talk or write about love while the people are grappling with depressing conditions of neo-colonialism and imperialism. For these writers, Africa must heed the words of Nkrumah and "seek first the political kingdom."

Furthermore, one wonders how the African writer would sound if he started to present love in a truly passionate sense. For, in keeping with his tradition and in keeping with literature which draws from the cultural experiences of his people, it is likely that the passionate love theme in African literature would sound phony, ridiculous and unconvincing to an African audience, though it may make a lot of sense to the west. Perhaps a good example of this is Ouologuem's *Bound to Violence*, where his presentation of love shocks the African reader and pleases the western one. Kane comments Ouologuem's concept of love in these words:

> In his work, Ouologuem has a concept of love which is atrocious: homosexuality which does not exist in our culture, all that vice, incest,

[11] Interview with Ezekiel Mphahlele by author, 1974.
[12] Mohammed Dib in Jean Déjeux, *Littérature Maghrébine de la langue française*, p. 155.
[13] Interview with Ngugi wa Thiong'o by author, 1974.
[14] Edgar Wright, *The Critical Evaluation of African Literature* (London: Heinemann, 1976), p. 114.

animality and so many things that belong to the white people or exist in whiteman's mind. But he put all these things with African characters which is false. The way he talked of love and hate is not characteristic of Africa.[15]

Perhaps it is only a matter of time before Africans begin producing works whose main theme will be exclusively love as they perceive it in their own world.

BIBLIOGRAPHY

ABRAHAMS, Peter. *Path of Thunder*. New York: Harper, 1948.

ACHEBE, Chinua. *A Man of the People*. New York: Doubleday, 1966.

_____ *No Longer at Ease*. Greenwich: Fawcett, 1969.

_____ *Things Fall Apart*. Greenwich: Fawcett, 1959.

BEIER, Ulli. *Introduction to African Literature*. Evanston: Northwestern University Press, 1967.

BETI, Mongo. *Mission terminée*. Paris: Correa, 1957.

BLAIR, Dorothy S. *African Literature in French*. Cambridge University Press, 1967.

BONI, Nazi. *Crépuscule des temps anciens*. Paris: Présence Africaine, 1962.

BONN, Charles. *La Littérature Algérienne de la langue française*. Ottawa: Naaman, 1974.

DATHORNE, O.R. *The Black Mind*. Minneapolis: University of Minnesota Press, 1974.

DEJEUX, Jean. *Littérature Maghrébine de langue française*. Ottawa: Naaman, 1973.

DIB, Mohammed. *Qui se souvient de la mer*. Paris: Seuil, 1962.

EKWENSI, Cyprian. People of the City. London: Heinemann, 1963.

FERAOUN, Mouloud. *Les Chemins qui montent*. Paris: Seuil, 1957.

GLEASON, Judith. *This Africa*. Evanston: Northwestern University Press, 1965.

HAZOUME, Paul. *Douguicimi*. Paris: Larousse, 1938.

_____ *L'Afrique littéraire et artistique*, No. 18, août 1971.

MPHAHLELE, Ezekiel. *African Writing Today*. London: Penguin, 1967.

NGUGI, James. *A Grain of Wheat*. London: Heinemann, 1967.

NWAPA, Flora. *Idu*. London: Heinemann, 1970.

ORTZEN, Len. *North African Writing*, London: Heinemann, 1970.

OUOLOGUEM, Yambo. *Le Devoir de violence*. Paris: Seuil, 1968.

QUENUM-BHELY, Olympe. *Un Piège sans fin*. Paris: Librairie Stock, 1960.

WRIGHT, Edgar. *The Critical Evaluation of African Literature*. London: Heinemann, 1976.

YACINE, Kateb. *Nedjma*. Paris: Seuil, 1956.

[15] Interview with Kane by author, 1972.

INDEPENDENCE AND DISILLUSION IN *LES SOLEILS DES INDEPENDENCES*: A NEW APPROACH

Fredric Michelman
Gettysburg College

A sense of disenchantment with the fruits of independence is not a new theme in African literature. In the last two decades, Africans writing in French and English have, in various ways, condemned a new black elite which, taking credit for the expulsion of the white colonizer and in the name of the "revolution," continues to exploit the masses through privilege, corruption and repression. A related theme has been the destructive force that colonialism and its aftermath have wrought on traditional societies. Both of these themes are present in Ahmadou Kourouma's *Les Soleils des Indépendances*[1], but what is unique about this fine novel lies not so much in *what* its author denounces as in the *manner* with which he does so. His style and point of view represent an especially happy departure from the linguistic orthodoxy and narrative approach so common to many francophone writers. In a rare interview, Kourouma deplores the "fetishism" surrounding the French language and the limiting effects that this has had on many African authors writing in that tongue. Speaking of his novel, he affirms, "I thought in Malinké and wrote it in French, taking liberties I consider natural with the classical language."[2] It is this fresh approach which I would briefly like to examine here. It might be helpful at the outset, however, to summarize the action of the novel, since, unfortunately, no English translation of it has yet appeared. (This, in spite of the fact, that it was awarded the "Prix de la revue *Etudes françaises*" in 1968 and has won considerable critical acclaim elsewhere.)[3]

Fama, a Malinké Muslim and hereditary prince of the traditional kingdom of Horodougou, has been deprived of his rightful position as chief by the French colonial administration. With the coming of independence, his activities as a trader are curtailed as well and, as the novel opens, we find him reduced to the humiliating role of "griot" or praise singer at Malinké funerals in the capital of the "Côte des Ebènes" (a lightly veiled name for Ivory Coast, the author's birthplace). His plight is all the more pitiable since his wife Salimata seems to be barren: in reality it is Fama who is sterile. Salimata, a very sensitively drawn character, has suffered deeply, having been traumatized as a young initiate by a painful excision ceremony followed by a brutal rape. In spite of this and her profound disappointment at being childless, she is a truly charitable soul and continues in her traditional rôle as a dutiful African wife. Fama is called back to his

---

[1] Montréal: Les Presses de L'Université de Montréal, 1968; Paris: Editions du Seuil, 1970; the translations are mine.

[2] Moncef S. Badday, "Ahmadou Kourouma, écrivain africain," *L'Afrique littéraire et artistique*, No. 10 (avril, 1970), p. 7.

[3] While this book (*Design and Intent...* was in press, a translation by Adrian Adams appeared. See: Kourouma, Ahmadou, *The Suns of Independence* (New York: Africana Publishing Co., 1981).

homeland for the funeral of his cousin Lancina, who had taken his place as chief. He, himself, is finally proclaimed chief in his native village of Togobala after some conflict with the representatives of the new single party. Fama returns to the capital with his dead cousin's youngest wife, Mariam (she is part of his inheritance) having every intention of returning to Togobala. Within a short time, however, he becomes implicated in a plot against the government, is arrested during a terrible wave of repression and is condemned to 20-years confinement in an atrocious prison camp. When the prisoners are unexpectedly released early, through an act of calculated clemency by the President, who turns the event into an orchestrated publicity stunt, Fama, disgusted and in failing health, shuns the festivities and boards a bus for Togobala. As the last representative of the Doumbouya dynasty, he is determined to fulfill the ancient prophesy and die in Horodougou.

Togobala is, however, located on the opposite side of the river forming the frontier between the Côte des Ebènes and the Socialist Republic of Nikinai (probably intended to be Guinea). Fama's realm of Horodougou spreads out on both sides of the artificially drawn border, which has been closed because of tension between the two nations. Enraged, Fama disobeys orders to stop, crosses the bridge separating them and jumps to the opposite bank where he is mortally wounded by a "sacred" crocodile. The prophesy has been fulfilled: Fama will be buried in the earth of his ancestors and the dynasty of the Doumbouya is extinguished forever.

Throughout the book, the misfortunes and sufferings of the hero (indeed, those of the whole people) are linked to what is seen by the hero as one underlying evil — Independence. This theme is, however, not presented in a single-minded and simplistic way, nor is it an exclusive one. Some readers will feel a certain ambiguity towards Fama who, nostalgic for his former royal privileges, is bitter at having been passed over in the distribution of the choice plums of Independence: government appointments guaranteed to enrich their holders. Fama, at the outset at least, is thus a somewhat suspect denigrator of the corrupt order. With time, however, he gains our sympathy and respect, assuming true heroic dimensions at the end. This ambivalent treatment of the hero and the progressive revelation of his integrity results in a psychological depth which, transcending the historical event, makes possible an eloquent commentary on the human condition. The same is true of the touchingly pathetic story of Salimata, which also carries with it an implied criticism of the status of African women. Our Western sensibility, at least, sees her subservient role and her and Mariam's treatment as objects to be passed on without their consent to brothers and cousins as a deplorable exploitation under modern circumstances. Given the extremely sympathetic portrayal of Salimata, this seems very likely the author's view as well.

The principal target of the book nevertheless remains, as its ironic title indicates, Independence. It should be understood, however, that it is not precisely Independence as such that is being excoriated here; we are witness rather to a profound sense of disappointment at the widespread betrayal of its bright promise. Colonialism had been the ultimate enemy and, indeed, Fama had taken part in the struggle to oust the White man. But, paradoxically, now that he has gone, some things are worse and nothing is better. For Fama, at least, there was freedom under the French to trade, an activity as vital to the Malinké as the air he breathes. With the coming of Independence, government-run cooperatives took over and put many traders, Fama being one of them, out of business. The other "swarm of locusts" which descended upon Africa hard on the heels of Independence is the single party, in Fama's words: "une bâtardise" (untranslatable, but something akin to "bastardy"); intruding itself into people's lives, destroying what tradition is left and, degradation of all degradations for Fama, Prince of Horodougou, the Party is run by sons of slaves. Reduced to "working" funerals as a griot, Fama laments:

> Fama Doumbouya! True Doumbouya, father a Doumbouya, mother a Doumbouya, last and legitimate descendent of the Doumbouya princes of Horodougou, totem panthers — he was a 'vulture'. A Doumbouya prince! A panther totem was running with hyenas. Ah! The suns of Independence! (p. 9)

A world gone awry. (Indeed, the traditional imagery of the sun as beneficial is reversed — these are "les soleils des Indépendances maléfiques," the evil suns of Independence [p. 9].) At a funeral he is attending, Fama is slapped by a griot. Shocked by the "bastardisation" of the Malinkés, he fears that "the shadow of the deceased will inform the spirits of the ancestors that, under the suns of Indépendence, Malinkés shame and even strike their prince" (p. 15). As for the chiefs in place, Independence and the Party have reduced them "to something worth no more than the droppings of a bird of prey" (p. 22). Returning to his native village, after a long absence, he finds it destitute, the buildings in disrepair, the inhabitants sickly. In his own compound, there are only two men capable of working the earth, and fourteen mouths to feed. "And the taxes, the Party assessments, and all the other bastardly monetary contributions demanded by Independence, where would *they* come from?" (p. 110)

Beyond attributing the material impoverishment evident in Togobala to the new party structure, Fama and his supporters also see it as an agent of division, undermining the cardinal values of his people, threatening them with extinction. During the showdown scene between the Party backers and those opposed to it, "the foreign [i.e. non-Malinké] delegate, not knowing Malinké customs, kept repeating himself, coming back to the same point again and again, irreconcilable, indomitable, like the penis of an enraged donkey. Fama was to — these were the orders and he would listen to no others — Fama was to kneel at the feet of the president of the committee, rub his lips against the ground and renounce his position, swear on the open Koran his faithfulness to the Party, to the committee and to the revolution." At this point, the narrator comments: "Let's be frank, this was about as likely to happen as his eating dog droppings." He goes on, "if things were to continue as they were going, humanism and brotherhood would disappear; no more balance of invisible forces who save the village, but rather hatred between families, the ire of the spirits, the curse of the ancestors" (p. 14).

Fama has already put in a word with those whom Birago Diop terms "the dead who are not dead": "Oh ancestors! great Doumbouyas! I will kill sacrifices for you, but all of you, with Allah's will, extirpate illegality, sterility, kill Independence and the single party, epidemics and clouds of locusts" (p. 121). This is a prayer that Fama will never see answered.

It is evident from some of the excerpts already quoted, that the language has a unique and non-Western flavor to it. The following images, at once concrete and poetic, like so many other throughout the novel, are firmly rooted in Africa's natural phenomena, in its soil, in its flora and fauna and often in its Malinké language itself. The morning "like any mother was beginning to give birth, very painfully, to the enormous harmattan sun" (p. 125). Fama's village "was poorer than the loincloth of the orphan, dried up like the river Touko at the height of the harmattan" (p. 131). "As for infidelity, huh, huh! honest women were becoming as rare in Houdougou as rams with one testicle" (p. 135). For two nights Fama cannot sleep, finding the idea of the upcoming palaver with the party committee "as uncomfortable as a boubou with too large a collar" (p. 136). The interminable greetings preceeding the palaver "lasted the time it takes a leper to thread a needle" (p. 138). When the floor was given to the president of the Party commit-tee, "sly son of a slave," he "moved through speech the way one walks through a marsh, feeling his way along, casting about questioning glances, gathering approval before going on" (p. 139). An irreverant image depicts a member of the French-educated elite who was, "like all young Malinkés just returned from France, impolite, like a ram sniffing at his mamma's hind-quarters" (p. 169). Seeking the reasons for Salimata's supposed sterility (as we have seen, it is in fact Fama who is sterile), Fama laments: "Her belly remained dry as granite, one could penetrate as deeply as one liked and excavate with the longest and strongest pick in order to plant a handful of the best seeds — all was swept away by a great river. Nothing would come of it" (p. 27). Beyond its effective utilization of the realities of local life and speech, this latter passage and others dealing with the same subject appear to symbolize the basic sterility of the entire male-dominated new order; it is conceivable even, that they constitute a subtle call for the recognition of the woman's potential in the elaboration of a truly new and just society. Finally, in addition to Malinké verbal imagery and proverbial sayings, we occasionally find the use of non-standard French, doubtlessly based on Malinké morphology and syntax: "Les Dahomées couchèrent nos femmes" (for "couchèrent avec") (p. 89); "Que Fama marie Mariam" (for "se marie avec") (p. 94); "nuitez" (for "passez la nuit") (p. 98).

But it is perhaps its point of view as much as its language and imagery which removes this work from the European model and lends to it a traditional, i.e. oral, quality. Although the point of view does shift often to Fama, the overall impress-ion given is one of a griot telling his story. The reader is constantly being addressed, "Let me hasten to tell [this story]" (p. 27), questioned (and answered), "Now tell me! Fama's trip to the capital (for a moon, according to him) — truly, tell me, was it really, really necessary? No and no!" (p. 151), treated as an accomplice, "We'll empty this old... hyena's bag later" (pp. 108-109), invited to celebrations (and here with a sly wink of the eye), "Because of the quivering of the girls' breasts, the pulsation of their buttocks and the whiteness of their teeth, let us avoid the dancers... Let us sit... in the hunters' area" (p. 149), instructed in local custom, "Why is it that Malinké celebrate the funeral on the fortieth day after burial? It is because..." (p. 143), and challenged,

"Who will contest this?" (p. 117).

Moreover, resemblances between the narrator of this novel and the traditional griot go beyond remarks addressed to his audience. It is on his, i.e. Malinké, terms and not on Western ones that we are shown the tragedy of independence. Why was there an insurrection against the government? It was inevitable "for the simple reason that the republics of the suns of Independence had not provided for such institutions as fetishes and sorcerers to stave off misfortune... Nothing happens without a previous sign" (pp. 160-161). In Horodougou, it is the oldest hyena of the mountains and a sacred boa (named "the Reverend") who announce the future to the living. But, asks the narrator, "where did one see the *koma* [devining ceremony], the hyena, the snake or the seer of the République des Ebènes? Nowhere. It was well known that the leaders of the suns of Independence often consulted deviners but for whom?... it was never for the community, never for the country but for themselves, to consolidate their own power" (p. 163). Moreover, all the tragic events which close the novel are seen first in dreams (carefully described) or have been predicted long before by the first ancestor of the Doumbouya. An air of fatality soars over the novel and, as it moves inexorably to its end, it takes on epic, even mythical, proportions. As Fama arrives at the closed border, the animals act strangely, sensing that something extraordinary is about to happen. In a scene that would be hard to equal in its violent intensity and beauty, Fama becomes an authentic tragic hereo, rising above his death, assuming true grandeur, becoming bigger than life. As Fama is attacked by the sacred crocodile, a border guard fires at the animal, wounding it mortally, "And as always in the Horodougou in such circumstances, it was the wild beasts who first understood the historic import of the cry of the man, the groaning of the animal, of the shot which had just broken the morning's peace" (p. 200). There ensues complete chaos with birds attacking men and animals who flee screaming into the forest. "The forest multiplied the echoes, setting off the winds which transported to the most remote villages and to the deepest tombs the cry that had just been uttered by the last of the Doumbouya" (p. 201.)

It is axiomatic that the written page can never capture the dynamic experience of an oral performance before a lively and participating group. But in *Les soleils des Indépendances* there is more than mere compromise. To be sure, this is not the first Francophone work to effectively use the griot narrator. Niane's *Sounjata* emphasizes this aspect of the narration, but this is, after all, a traditional epic and not a novel. Ouologuem employs this technique in *Le devoir de violence* but does so in a much less sustained manner than Kourouma. The author of *Les soleils des Indépendances*, while moulding the raw clay of foreign words in an alien form (the novel), has nevertheless succeeded in imparting a vibrantly African oral quality to his written prose. This is no mean feat and should be seen as an encouraging development in the African declaration of cultural independence.

SOYINKA'S *SEASON OF ANOMY*:
OFEYI'S QUEST

Obi Maduakor
University of Nigeria, Nsukka

Season of Anomy (1973) is an intensely religious book both in its preoccupation with moral issues and the strong impact of its ritual undertone. The imagination that conceived it is nurtured by the same moral outrage that occasioned the October poems of *Idanre and Other Poems* (1967) and most of the elegies in *A Shuttle in the Crypt* (1972).

One does not have to venture far into *Season of Anomy* to encounter passages with a note of pathos and moral indignation similar to what we find in the two verse collections mentioned above.[1] Soyinka's moral imagination became even more sensitive, more outraged after his experiences in prison. The declaration in *The Man Died* (1972) that "For me, justice is the first condition of humanity"[2] sounds like an ethical manifesto.

One of the consequences of his increasing dedication to the cause of justice is that the world of his postwar imaginative writings is frequently dominated by visionary seekers. We encounter these pilgrims early in the poems of *A Shuttle in the Crypt*.

The quest motif that is so insistent in *A Shuttle* attains a climactic dimension in *Season of Anomy*. There are of course earlier reminders of the image of the seeker in Soyinka's own works, such as Sekoni and his obsessions with the universal dome of existence in *The Interpreters* (1965), and the Professor with his quasi-mystical and quasi-magical groping for the Word in *The Road* (1965). But neither in *The Interpreters* nor in *The Road* is the quest theme developed on as grand a scale or explored with so complex an interplay of allegory and myth as we find it in *Season of Anomy*.

The quest theme in the later work runs on at least two levels; one is social and the other is personal. The two dimensions are interrelated, for each reinforces the other. Ofeyi the social reformer is also the archetype of all eternal voyagers and all lone seekers. If allegory is the language of the social dimension of the quest, myth is the idiom of its personal dimension.

On the social level, the quest is related to what might be described as a moral alternative for a nation in a state of anomy. It is suggested in *The Man Died*[3] that the Nigeria of the era of civil war might have been spared much bitterness and much suffering if it had given change to the mediatory initiative of a revolutionary movement whose inspiration was ethical. The ethical qualification is crucial, for it

---

[1] See the poems "Massacre, October '66" in *Idanre and Other Poems* (London: Methuen, 1967), pp. 51-52, and "Conversation at Night with a Cockroach" in *A Shuttle in the Crypt* (New York: Hill and Wang, 1972), pp. 5-13.

[2] Wole Soyinka, *The Man Died* (London: Rex Collings, 1972), p. 95.

[3] See chapters Two, Twelve, and Twenty-Three.

is on such a moral absolute, Soyinka implies, that a new national solidarity which transcends ethnic and religious loyalties could be founded. Victor Banjo was for Soyinka a one-time hero of such a movement. He is remembered in *A Shuttle* in the poem entitled "And What of it if Thus He Died?"

Victor Banjo's Third Force[4] was short-lived, but the idea behind the movement persists in Soyinka and in his character Ofeyi. Explaining the Shage project to Zaccheus, who is possessed of beauty of soul though utterly lacking in heroic aspirations, Ofeyi says:

> "New projects like the Shage Dam meant that we could start with newly created working communities. New affinities, working-class kinships as opposed to the tribal. We killed the atavistic instinct once and for all in new ventures like Shage."[5]

The method advocated in *Season of Anomy* for the transformation of society differs from what Victor Banjo had contemplated. Banjo was to have relied on military operations by virtue of the nature of the emergency that existed in Nigeria at the time he emerged on the national scene. Ofeyi, on the other hand, desires to carry out a quiet revolution, relying essentially on the "trick of conversion," that is, on a subtle incursion into the territories of the human heart.

The example of the agricultural community of Aiyéré appealed to Ofeyi as a social solidarity founded upon values that were humane and spiritual. In Aiyéré rituals still function as a symbolic affirmation of man's indebtedness to the forces of nature; ceremonies of renewal are frequently enacted; familiar images of rebirth in Soyinka's iconography such as camwood, chalk, and oil feature in the invocations to the dead; and dawn remains the hour of communion with the divine. Aiyéré is typical of the moral order that Ofeyi seeks. But he has first to master its heartbeat, to thoroughly understand its essence before he may transmit its values to his own society. One way by which he may understand the Aiyéré idea is to come to terms with those nonsexual values which Iriyise embodies, for Iriyise is earth, the symbolic mother earth that had appeared in the personality of Oya in the long poem "Idanre." In one moment of insight Ofeyi recognizes Iriyise's identity with the soil of Aiyéré. "She took to Aiyéré," he notices, "as a new organism in search of its true element" (p. 3). Iriyise's function as an embodiment of the creative potency of earth is not lost on the people of Aiyéré. The women readily identify her personaly with forces that encourage growth and vegetation. "Her fingers spliced wounded saplings with the ease of a natural healer. Her presence...inspired the rains" (p. 20).

Iriyise is linked, then, with the agricultural world of Aiyéré and, by extension, with the spiritual values of that world. For there is a strong sympathy in the book

---

[4] Victor Banjo was the Commander of the Biafran Forces that overran the old Midwestern Region of Nigeria (now Bendel State) in the early months of the Nigerian Civil War. He was also the leader of a revolutionary movement, The Third Force, whose political ideology was socialist. The Third Force, was opposed to the Biafran/secession; it was strongly in favour of a united Nigeria run by men of proven ability and integrity. The social anomy of the war years was a justification of the intention of the Third Force to seize power and establish a socialist regime in the country. This appears to have been the original intention of the January 1966 military coup.

[5] Wole Soyinka, *Season of Anomy* (London: Rex Collings, 1973), p. 170; subsequent references are to this edition and will appear in the text.

between land and the moral priorities of the people that inhabit it. Even in Ilosa where Iriyise is pod, the exploration of the resources of the land by the Cartel is spoken of as the "*outrage of the Pod*" (p. 48; my italics). But Iriyise's role as the personification of what Soyinka would call the spirit of revolutionary dare is probably more important.[6] She encapsulates the virtues of energy and motion, as well as the positive forces of social change. The Dentist's appraisal of her in this regard is significant. He sees her as a "touch and standard-bearer, super-mistress of universal insurgence. To abandon such political weapon in any struggle is to admit to lack of foresight. Or Imagination" (p. 219).

The Dentist[7] himself is also a protagonist of change. But his ethic of indiscrimate assassination is rejected on moral grounds. His obsessions with a concept of sheer violence link him with Chief Batoki or Zaki Amuri, whereas it is the point of the novel that Ofeyi's humane, almost religious approach towards social problems should be distinguished from the brutal means by which the Cartel oligarchy imposes the dictatorship of the privileged few on an unwilling many. "When you eliminate, you have in mind something to follow," Ofeyi tells the Dentist, "something to replace what you eliminate. Otherwise your action is negative and futile" (p. 111).

Iriyise is a more acceptable agent, not only for the fact that her revolutionary impulse is under Ofeyi's control, but also because she operates through a strategy of disguise as is noticeable in her performance in the melodramatic Pandora's Box episode or in the more subtle dance at Shage. Furthermore, she is qualified by her spiritual affinities with Aiyéré to effect change with Aiyéré itself. For Ofeyi is critical of Aiyéré as an esoteric hinterland. Aiyéré is meaningful only when the values that inform it can be made to replace the ethos of a materialistic society. For this reason the Asian girl Taiila is ultimately rejected as Ofeyi's companion in the quest. Taiila is the personification of the placid will, the serene spirit of conformity. She is imagined as an "insulated oasis of peace," a "still centre" that shies away from tragic encounter with "outer chaos" (pp. 238-40) She lacks the "caged tigress' in Iriyise. She is Aiyéré as Pa Ahime conceives it — her family is described as a microcosm of Aiyéré (p. 238). Iriyise, on the other hand, stands for the reformed image of Aiyéré which Ofeyi is endeavoring to create, that is, a more assertive, more militant and evangelical Aiyéré whose values should be extended beyond its boundaries.

Shage is important as Aiyéré's most crucial contact with that outside world

[6] Iriyise fulfills several roles in the novel. She stands for the image of woman as earth, as mother, as a lover, and as a muse. As an earth-mother, she is the Cocoa Princess. She appears in most of the posters advertising the alimentary values of cocoa food products. As Cocoa Princess, she accompanies Zaccheus and his Cocoa Bean Orchestra in their commercial tours throughout the country. She disapproves of the Cartel's exploitation of the resources of the land, and shares Ofeyi's passion for social reform which will ensure an equitable distribution of the resources of the land. She appreciates Aiyéré's social order because it guarantees such a just distribution, and because it is founded on reverence for the creative benevolence of earth which she embodies. She is also the object of Ofeyi's quest — a quest for a just society and for a woman who is both a muse and a lover.

[7] The Dentist's real name is Isola Demakin. He is Aiyéré's secret agent, both at home and abroad. Ofeyi discovered the Dentist's links with Aiyéré late in the novel (p. 216). He came into contact with Ofeyi during one of his missions abroad. The Dentist claims to have studied dentistry but Dentist is a nickname by which he is known outside Aiyéré circles. His habit of speaking of the elimination by assassination of corrupt public servants in terms of dental extraction earned him the name.

which is represented by the universe of the Cartel. The initial success of Aiyéré's operations at Shage is a personal triumph for Iriyise. Her dance of the young shoot sought to reenact the process of sowing, germination, and budding. The dance soon becomes a mystical experience, transforming her person into a blossoming shoot. Last in its rhythmic sensation, she sprouts "leaves and fresh buds from neck and fingers, shaking her hair free of dead leaves and earth and absorbing light and air through every pore" (p. 41). As a goddess of earth, she is capable of reactivating the recreative energies of earth that lay dormant in Shage. The dance combines neatly the double sense of shoot as seed and idea. The Shage earth is favorable for the growth of the vegetational seed as well as the ideological seed. But Shage is also the scene of the Cartel's most deadly assault on forces of renewal in both the human and natural realms. The success of the Cartel's operations of destruction at Shage plunges Ofeyi into one of his visionary moments. As he contemplates the ruins of Shage, his mind conjures up an immense chasm of nonbeing as a universal grave for desecrated humanity. The underworld has consistently functioned as a mirror image of the actual world inhabited by doomed humanity. Such is the implication of the entombed existence of the church at the Tabernacle of Hope and of the graveyard metaphor fo the mortuary episode. At Shage Ofeyi sees "where the rest of mankind had rushed, and how his was the only consciousness observing the dark pulsating chasms of tearing, grasping, clawing gorging humanity" (p. 176). Ofeyi's role is to heal, to infuse new life into a flesh where the "blood...had caked.'"[8] But at Shage he sought in vain to invoke Ahime's scalpel of light and life on the ravines of death and waste, to inundate the chasms of nonbeing with sympathetic bleeding from the bull's elixir.

After the Shage debacle, the Aiyéré idea returns to its source, but according to the Dentist, the journey back marks the route for a more definite return.

But the quest does not terminate with the search for Iriyise. It will go on, as Ofeyi discloses (p. 242), even after Iriyise has been found. Man's eternal restlessness, Soyinka wrote,[9] is always symbolized in a search. At this point the quest theme embraces more fundamental and more personal issues, such as the artist's quest for self-knowledge, his search for beauty in its relation to art, the search for truth in its ontological context, and, for emotional ballast to steady a mind in turmoil. Those other quests are summed up by Ofeyi in one important statement: "....every man feels the need to seize for himself the enormity of what is happening, of the time in which it is happening. Perhaps deep down I realize that the search would immerse me in the meaning of the event, lead me to a new understanding of history" (p. 218).

From whatever angle one views the quest, it is, by Ofeyi's understanding of it, a tragic undertaking. "Mire and mud, for some these are the paths to beauty and peace" (pp. 97-98), he tells Taiila. This other remark to Taiila is equally revealing: "I also seek beauty, but that kind which has been tested and stressed" (p. 99). Ofeyi, the mythic explorer, must pass through a mythic landscape, a landscape of grottos and tunnels, of stunted scrublands and hyenas, cats and vultures, which are

[8] *A Shuttle*, p. 9.

[9] Wole Soyinka, "From a Common Black Cloth: A Reassessment of the African Literary Image," *The American Scholar*, 32 (1963), p. 392.

symbolic representations of the ordeals of the questing pilgrim. To overcome these obstacles, Ofeyi relies increasingly on the restorative potency of rituals. He frequently evokes Ahime at moments of spiritual crisis, for he has come to associate Ahime's ceremonial scalpel with restorative essences. Thus, after his first major encounter with the agents of the Cartel (Chapters III-V), Ofeyi retreats to Aiyéré's bowered sanctuary for spiritual rehabilitation. He has to retreat thither for Aiyéré is a resting-place for all combatants engaged in the battles of the world. Ahime explains: "After all the battles of the world, one needs a resting-place. And often, in between the battles. Aiyéré was created for such needs" (p. 28). On this occasion, however, the restorative powers within the sanctuary speak to him of failure. The cleansing rite he performs at Labbe Bridge is more rewarding. Nature herself participates in the ritual of cleansing. The egrets "picked him clean of blood-infesting ticks," and the waters "shut his ears to all cacophony, his nostrils to pollution, transmitting only the rhythm of cropping and quiet germination" (p. 195). The water reeds evoke memories of Ahime's healing hands. They whisper healing "incantations over a child in agony" (p. 195). Their healing vibrances stand in sharp contrast with the death exhalations emitted by the Cartel's machinery of destruction.

It is a feature of the novel that Aiyéré should be viewed from a perspective of contrast with the universe inhabited by the agents of the Cartel. The juxtaposition of two worlds with two diversely opposed moral orders tends to resolve the tensions within the novel into an allegorical conflict between good an evil. The allegorical polarization plots the graph of the novel's symbolic structure. The voyager Ofeyi advances from the pastoral enclaves of Aiyére to the scenes of conflict represented by Cross-river who is the best illustration of the impact on characterization of the author's allegorical imagination. Aliyu is simply an embodiment of the "metaphysic [sic] condition called evil" (p. 276). His physical distortions reinforce the absolute deformity of mind among his Cross-river compatriots; but the use of Aliyu as an allegorical medium is ironical since he himself is not evil.

Landscape sustains more successfully the burden imposed on it by the allegorical technique; it operates primarily on a functional basis. As noted before, the condition of the land reflects the moral character of the people who inhabit it. Aiyéré's ceremony of renewal is replaced in Cross-river by a deadly ritual whose libations paint a "testament of damnation on earth" (p. 141). In Cross-river earth is smeared with human brains and with the entrails of female wombs. The enormity of the crime committed on land and life is suggested by an allusion to the biblical apocalypse "...this is the fifth face of the Apocalypse...the plague of rabid dogs."

Within such a physical and spiritual wasteland, the Aiyéré idea maintains a precarious existence as a glimmer of light shining in the darkness. The underground church at the Tabernacle of Hope is a refuge for those who live in fear. The priest's "path-finding form" (p. 271) is truly the Way. Religion is the final hope of salvation for those who live in the darkness of terror. It is at the Tabernacle that Taiila fulfills herself as a messenger of love and peace. Her humanity is aroused by the condition of the dead and dying. Her place is ultimately with situations of suffering, and not with the revolutionary spirit that questions and challenges.

Of the two dimensions of the quest already discussed, it is in the second, that is, in its role as the effort of the human spirit to comprehend itself that the novel is likely to make a more permanent impact. Amos Tutuola has given us a folkloric version of this form of quest in *The Palm-Wine Drinkard* (1952), and Camara Laye has explored its implications in the tradition of Kafka in *The Radiance of the King* (1956); but Soyinka's technique is more sophisticated and more complicated than Tutuola's or Laye's. His seasoned approach represents a major advance in the growth of the African novel.

THE CHILD-NARRATOR AND THE THEME
OF LOVE IN MONGO BETI'S
LE PAUVRE CHRIST DE BOMBA

Abioseh Mike Porter
University of Alberta

Critical commentary on Mongo Beti's *Le Pauvre Christ de Bomba*[1] has been concerned, above all, with elaborating upon the obvious themes of anti-clericalism and colonial oppression, and to a lesser extent with elucidating the narrative skills of the author.[2] One might have thought that little more remains to be said on this early Beti novel, but since that novelist's *Perpétue*[3] appeared in 1974 a new question which has important implications for criticism of *Le Pauvre Christ de Bomba* and, perhaps, of Beti's other early works poses itself. Is the theme of love which has been seen by critics as such a dominant theme in *Perpétue* not a theme that had previously been important in Beti's *oeuvre*, and overlooked by critics?

At first, *Perpétue* does appear to be a new departure. It lacks the first person point of view of the most commented upon earlier novels, yet it is, at least, as complex as the ironically-related tales, *Le Pauvre Christ de Bomba* and *Mission terminée*. Furthermore, it deals with problems of women as the privileged vehicle for anti-imperialist subject matter; and again, this marks a difference. But if we can assert that Beti has developed his skill and has modified part of a recurring though unnoticed subject rather than just pursuing new ones, and that the grimness that saturates *Perpétue* was always a major point beneath the humour of the surface in some of the earlier works, then it becomes tempting to assert some thematic continuity in Beti. This means re-reading such major pieces as *Le Pauvre Christ de Bomba* and *Mission terminée* from the fresh perspective of *Perpétue* to see whether or not the theme of love is actually a continuous and revived theme which has been largely neglected in the criticism of the Beti novels of the pre-

---

[1] Mongo Beti, *Le Pauvre Christ de Bomba*, (Paris: Présence Africaine, 1976). This novel was originally published by Laffont in Paris, 1956. Page references are, however, to the 1976 edition which shall be abbreviated as *PCB*.

[2] The anti-clerical and anti-colonial themes have been treated by various critics, among whom the following can be cited: Thomas Melone, *Mongo Beti: L'homme et le destin* (Paris: Présence Africaine, 1971); Thomas Cassirer, "The Dilemma of Leadership as Tragi-comedy in the novels of Mongo Beti," *L'Esprit Créateur* 10 (1970), 223-33; William Umezinwa, "Révolte et création artistique dans l'oeuvre de Mongo Beti," *Présence Francophone* 10 (1975), 35-48. Beti's stylistic virtuosity, especially in his use of irony, has also been mentioned in various articles: Kwabena Britwum, "Irony and the Paradox of Idealism in Mongo Beti's *Le Pauvre Christ de Bomba*," *Re: Arts and Letters* 6 ii (1972), 48-68; Fernando Lambert, "L'ironie et l'humour de Mongo Beti dans *Le Pauvre Christ de Bomba*," *Etudes Littéraires* 7 (1974), 381-94; Eustace Palmer, *An Introduction to the African Novel* (New York: Africana Publishing Corp., 1972. Although Palmer's chapter on Beti is devoted to *Mission to Kala*, his penetrating analysis of Beti's style can be applied to *Le Pauvre Christ de Bomba*.

[3] Mongo Beti, *Perpétue* (Paris: Buchet & Chastel, 1974).

independence era.[4] For my present purposes, however, I shall concentrate on *Le Pauvre Christ de Bomba* — a novel whose events are brilliantly recounted by a first person child-narrator.

In *Le Pauvre Christ de Bomba*, there are several love relationships. The reader can distinguish institutionalized ones like that between Zacharie and his wife, Clementine, illicit rapports such as those between the *sixa* women and some men associated with the church, and the youthful liaison between Denis and Catherine. However, the best demonstration of the theme of love and of its importance, not only in the world of the acolyte-narrator but also in the novel as a whole, is seen in the affective relationships between Denis and le père Drumond, on the one hand, and between the young boy and Catherine, on the other.

In order to illustrate this, I shall divide the novel into two sections corresponding to these two relationships. The first part starts from the time Denis is handed over to the mission authorities, and ends with the beginning of the sexual experiences. The rest of the novel obviously constituted the second part. In the earlier section, le père Drumond's paternalism leads Denis to develop a strong infatuation (which the boy interprets as filial love) for him. Denis remarks that whereas le père Le Guen, the other priest in the mission appears to him as a friend, le père Drumond becomes more like a father. It is this attachment to the holy man, which becomes even more prominent when one realizes that Denis has virtually been abandoned by his only living parent, his father, that makes the young boy become such a faithful lackey. It is, however, a sign of Beti's craftsmanship that he carefully weaves in this theme dealing with basic human relationships while developing the more popular or topical themes in the work.

Beti seems to be hinting that love for our fellow human beings should include the ability not only to acknowledge the virtues but also to tolerate and correct the vices of our loved ones. As a consequence, the novelist demonstrates that uncritical, adultory love directed at a single individual leads to blindness and stupidity, as we see in the many instances involving Denis and "le pauvre Christ" Drumond; the young boy gives unequivocal support to Drumond, no matter what he does: Denis endorses the "punishment" meted out by the priest to the Tala people; he disapproves of Drumond's well-deserved nickname, "Le malin," and he has nothing but disdain for the young man whose fiancée has been impounded by the church, and who therefore questions the man of God about the legitimacy of such an action. The "love" Denis has for Drumond simply allows him to live in a self-deluding world, and as a result he often ratifies some of the most morally outrageous actions taken by his mentor, and for which we know the author is obviously condemning the Reverend Father. For instance, when Drumond unsympathetically rejects the old, toothless and penniless Christian woman who could not afford to pay her church dues, Denis' initial reaction is one of enthusiastic

---

[4] Robert P. Smith, Jr., "Mongo Beti: The Novelist Looks at Independence and the Status of the African Woman," *College Language Association Journal* XIX 3 (1976), 301-11. Smith postulates that the grimness of *Perpétue*, unlike Beti's previous novels, shows "the seriousness of purpose and manner which the themes of politics and status of women demand of the author...," and that through this non-comic treatment of themes a new Beti has emerged. This paper will not take up that debate; instead it will read an earlier work with the fresh optics of *Perpétue*, since we know from experience that new books of substance often turn out, in essence, to be re-writings of previous works.

support; however, as the scene progresses one notices that this support becomes more and more skeptical. This makes one suspect that Denis realizes the basic unchristian quality of Drumond's action but only lends support to such an action because it is done by his "father." It is for this reason that I do not think, as Kwabena Britwum suggests, that Denis maintains "an unwitting ironic distance" here, or that it is only father Drumond who receives Beti's gibes.[5]

The reader also notices that the priest's religious frenzy is not only grotesque but can also be dangerous, hence one sees the high premium he attaches to the "spiritual" side of life when he is called to offer aid to Joseph Garba, the villager who has been impaled by a tree; even though the spiritual father is summoned to give physical help to this seriously-injured man, Father Drumond's only concern is with the spiritual, and thus the only assistance he renders is to ask the man for confession. Joseph Garba dies, and from Denis the Reverend gets the warmest commendation for the part Drumond plays:

> J'étais heureux en songeant que cet événement les remettrait peut-être dans le droit chemin. Et peut-être, si les gens s'amendaient, le R.P.S. ne renoncerait pas à ce beau pays. (*PCB* p. 42).
>
> (I was happy thinking that this event would perhaps put them on the right path again. And perhaps, if the people mend their ways, the R.F.S. will not renounce this beautiful country.) Translation mine.

The boy expresses similar satisfaction and hope when he learns that the colonial administration will forcibly eject people from their homes and conscript them for forced labour; the people will not only learn their lesson about God but will go quickly to the man the narrator loves so well, le père Drumond. It comes to us as no surprise, therefore, that he almost leaps for joy when the church leader launches an unjustified attack on the village dancers, and when he humiliates Sanga Boto, the charlatan traditional healer.

In each of these scenes, Beti is turning his ironic focus from one aspect of colonial life to another and at the same time directing it at the narrator. Such a narrative strategy is largely possible not simply because of the narrator's *innocence* but also because of the "love" Denis has from Drumond. The novelist makes the point that as long as Denis maintains this narrow relationship with Drumond, or any other person for that matter, his vision of the external realities of the world will remain befogged. Such a perspective allows the writer to use stylistic devices such as double irony when commenting on the relationships between people.

The relationship between Denis and Catherine in the second section confirms the opinion that Mongo Beti does not view genuine love as a sentiment blindly directed at a single person. This is the main reason why the sexual encounter between Denis and Catherine becomes the pivotal point for the transition of Denis' infatuation for le père Drumond to something close to love for the priest, Catherine and other people. Furthermore, focus on the relationship between the two young people facilitates the interpretation of *Le Pauvre Christ de Bomba* as a work

---

[5] Britwum is one of the critics who at times fails to see the double-edged irony employed by Beti. This use of irony is mainly brought about by Denis' "love" for Drumond.

dealing with "education" or "initiation" and its connection to social forces.[6]

One can give an almost stage by stage documentation of Denis' coming into awareness from the moment he has his first sexual experience with Catherine. In this section, Beti is not suggesting that sex is synonymous with love, but he certainly seems to be hinting that raw sex (which can be a very objective act), is closer to love than the obsequious devotion, full of self-effacement, that Denis had hitherto displayed. We notice that from a youthful initiating encounter, real love begins to develop between Denis and Catherine in this situation, and the stupidity and blindness which had characterized Denis' points of view on previous occasions become increasingly replaced by clarity and open-mindedness. It is true that the boy is still loyal to Father Drumond even after his sexual initiation, but Beti makes the narrator also realize that infatuation or even an abstraction such as "divine love" which excludes the possibility for worldly love for people is a pure chimera promoted by oppressors and should therefore not be regarded as love.

It is not surprising, therefore, that as Denis' idea of real love starts growing, his overall attitude to people changes; he becomes more sympathetic and understanding and thus, unlike on previous occasions when the Priest's attack on the people would have received Denis' complete assent, the young boy now begins to see validity in Zacharie's skepticism towards his patron's fanatical, proselytizing mission. He wonders whether Zacharie might not, after all, be right in maintaining this critical attitude. We get glimpses of mental growth here, and the child-narrator is on his way to self-illumination, but he is still not free from the ironic barbs of the author, since he still hopes the Reverend Father Superior will stay and "save" his people; the collusion between the church and the oppressive state machinery is still not very clear to him.

As the story progresses, however, one notices the acolyte's waning interest in his religious obligations; he shows little enthusiasm for, and even dodges serving mass at Zibi and Akamba respectively. While still at Akamba, Denis agrees with the village catechist that Sango Boto's supporters are afraid of the devil just as the church's followers are scared of God's vengeance. These views, which put God and the devil on the same footing, would have been scorned by Denis prior to his initiation to the mysteries of the flesh and to the beginning of genuine affective feelings for people. This process of dereification continues and he sums up his previous status neatly when he realizes what had been going on in the *sixa*.

> J'ai toujours entendu dire que les femmes de la sixa avaient une mauvaise conduite et *je n'en croyais rien...Dieu suis-je bête!* C'est toujours la même histoire: *Il se passe des tas de choses et moi je ne vois jamais rien.* (*PCB* pp. 160-161)
>
> I always heard it rumoured that the women in the sixa led a bad life and *I never believed a thing...My God, how stupid have I been!* It's always the same story: *so many things happen and I never see a thing.* (Translation and emphasis are mine.)

---

[6] Both Cassirer and Lambert (above, note 2) make references to the process of "education" or "initiation" that takes place in the novel. They do not, however, bring out the direct link between the "love" relationship of the first part contributes to a very effective use of irony, so does the increasingly broader, more humane kind of love (demonstrated by Denis and Catherine in the second part), lead the boy to a greater awareness of the harsh realities of life.

When one notices that in these latter incidents (such as the "revelations" in the sixa, Denis rushes neither to defend Drumond nor to condemn the people, one realizes that the young boy has been greatly enlightened. This enlightenment is, to a large extent, enhanced by Denis' rapport with Catherine. He has now received a taste of and acquired a feel for sex and love, and there is the strong suggestion that these make him come to terms with the world. The scales which had previously been placed over his eyes by the "love" he had for Drumond are removed, and little wonder that Denis feels as if he had just awakened out of a sleeping state when they return to Bomba after their tour.

The development of the narrator's perception is shown in its final stage on his coming back to Bomba. He admits that he had been unduly severe in judging the Tala people and he finally expresses unreserved doubts about the efficacy of the christian religion. Although Denis' option of going to work for a Greek merchant is far from the best one, we are left with the positive hope that his view of the world in general and of affective relationships in particular will be more reasonable. It is also safe to say that at the end of the story Denis has realized his error of giving blind, adultory love to one person, and we cannot imagine him indulging in that kind of activity again. What we can imagine, however, is his participation in real, humane love, having been introduced to its possibility by Catherine.

Looking at some works that have come out of Cameroon, one notices that the theme of love has been recurrent, though unnoticed. It plays a major role in Ferdinand Oyono's *Une vie de boy*.[7] where the hero Toundi's "education" comes largely as a result of his knowing too much about the adulterous affairs of his master's wife. Love and marriage are the dominant themes also of Guillaume Oyônô-Mbia's *Trois prétendants, un mari*,[8] Francis Bebey's *Le Fils d'Agatha Moudio*,[9] Mbella Sonne Dipoko's *Because of Women*,[10] and, as has been previously mentioned, *Perpétue*. This seems to suggest that the treatment of the affective relationships between people has come to form a good part of the tradition of Cameroonian literature, and for Beti, this theme which he handles with such finesse in *Perpétue*, is one he had subtly treated even as relatively early as 1956 in *Le Pauvre Christ de Bomba*.

[7] Ferdinand Oyono, *Une vie de boy* (Paris: Julliard, 1956).

[8] Guillaume Oyônô-Mbia, *Trois prétendants, un mari* (Yaounde: Editions CLE, 1967).

[9] Francis Bebey, *Le Fils d'Agatha Moudio* (Yaounde: Editions CLE, 1967).

[10] Mbella Sonne Dipoko, *Because of Women* (London: Heinemann, 1969.)

EXTRA-CONTINENTAL

THE USE OF AFRICAN LITERATURE IN ANTHROPOLOGY COURSES

Nancy J. Schmidt

Harvard University

Anthropology aims to study all aspects of human behavior, yet the discipline is still tied to its origin as the study of non-literate people.[1] Whereas the scope of anthropology has been widened in recent years to cover many aspects of mid-twentieth century life among formerly non-literate people, such as schooling, urbanization, and economic development, written literature still is not a major, or even a minor topic of anthropological concern.

Only a handful of American anthropologists list written literature as one of their special areas of interest;[2] no departments that offer a concentration in anthropology have a special program in written literature;[3] the only guide to resources for teaching anthropology sponsored by the American Anthropological Association does not include literature as a subtopic;[4] and a recent review of innovative teaching in anthropology edited by the past president of the American Anthropological Association makes no reference to teaching about written literature.[5]

To date there is only one general anthropology text that focuses on literature, *Anthropology Through Literature*.[6] Both its title and contents reflect the primary interest of anthropologists in literature — "to help readers understand the concepts and data of anthropology through the medium of literature."[7] The editors of this

---

[1] The statements in this paper are about American anthropology. Whereas written literature is not a topic of substantial concern to either British or French anthropologists, I am not familiar with course syllabi in these countries.

[2] Hans H. Leder, California State at Fullerton, literature; Alvin H. Morrison, SUNY College at Fredonia, anthropology and literature; Denise O'Brien, Temple University, anthropological fiction; Charles F. Urbanowica, California State at Chico, anthropological fiction; Carlos Velez, UCLA, anthropology of literature, and the author who lists African literature as one of three special areas of interest. Anthropologists who teach in institutions that do not offer a concentration in anthropology are not included in the *Guide to Departments of Anthropology* from which this information was obtained.

[3] American Anthropological Association. *Guide to Departments of Anthropology 1978-79*. Washington, D.C.: American Anthropological Association, 1978. This guide includes only U.S. and Canadian departments that offer either an undergraduate or graduate concentration in anthropology; thus it does not include all departments where anthropology is taught.

[4] David G. Mandelbaum, Gabriel Lasker and Ethel M. Alberta. *Resources for the Teaching of Anthropology*. Washington, D.C.: American Anthropological Association, Memoir 95, 1963.

[5] "Anthropology," in "Report on Teaching," *Change* 10, 1 (1978), 6-27.

[6] James P. Spradley and George E. McDonough, eds. *Anthropology Through Literature*. Boston: Little, Brown, 1973. Of the thirty-nine literary excerpts in this volume, three were written by two African authors, Chinua Achebe and Nadine Gordimer. Three additional excerpts about Africa come from autobiographical or popularly written works by anthropologists. This exemplifies the lack of a clear definition of literature and the disregard for the creative aspects of fiction by the editors.

[7] Ibid. p. xii.

text and other anthropologists who use written literature in their courses find literature especially useful in teaching because it provides a "sensitivity...often missing in conventional anthropological writing" and includes "the wholeness and vividness of life, the immediate experience the anthropologist knew in the field" that is lost when anthropologists write monographs phrased in abstract categories and relationships between them.[8] Literature shows the "inner world of the actors" which anthropological monographs seldom do.[9] It is not an accident that almost every excerpt in the text focuses on culture change and an individual's response to it, since this has been a use of written documents by anthropologists for two generations.[10]

Introductory texts on Africa prepared by anthropologists usually ignore written literature.[11] Melville Herskovits was unique among anthropologists in the 1960s in mentioning literature in *The Human Factor in Changing Africa* as part of the educational context, as an aspect of nationalistic cultural expression, as part of changes occurring in the arts, as well as a source of thematic analysis for learning about changing African values.[12] But Melville Herskovits was quite unique among

[8] Ibid. p. xii and xiii. This idea is developed more specifically by Langness and Frank who state: "We judge an ethnographic novel by the quality of the authorial voice, by the aptness or pungency of detail, by the consistency of the characters and their culture, and by the plausibility of their behavior as situations develop in which the reader becomes more equipped to assess the characters' attitudes and choices. These descriptions must be corroborated by outside reports for us to believe that their reality is substantial, rather than a chimera..." L.L. Langness and Gelya Frank, "Fact, Fiction and the Ethnographic Novel," *Anthropology and Humanism Quarterly* 3, 1-2 (1978), 20.

[9] Spradley and McDonough, *Anthropology Through Literature*, p. xv.

[10] Although the editors do not mention the ideas of Clyde Kluckhohn, he recommended the use of personal documents in anthropology, which included autobiography, biography, and fictional autobiography and biography among others, to overcome the weaknesses of standard ethnography. "Until anthropologists can deal rigorously with the 'subjective factors' in the lives of 'primitives' their works will be flat and insubstantial." Although Kluckhohn had no interest in written literature per se and was not an africanist, he suggested that Mofolo's *Chaka* was an important ethnographic document, despite its being largely imaginary, because it was written by an African in an African language. Clyde Kluckhohn, *The Personal Document in Anthropological Science. Social Science Research Council Bulletin* 53 (1945), 162 and 84. Margaret Mead coordinated research during World War II that used written literature, along with other products of expressive culture, as a source of thematic analysis about character types and cultural values for societies where fieldwork was not possible. This type of research was not continued after the war. See Margaret Mead and Rhoda Metraux, eds. *The Study of Culture at a Distance*. Chicago: University of Chicago, 1953, Part 5: "Written and Oral Literature." Both Kluckhohn and Mead, as well as psychological anthropologists today occasionally use written literature to obtain data on social roles and on personality factors.

[11] For example, the leading text of the 1960s, Simon and Phoebe Ottenberg, eds. *Cultures and Societies of Africa*. New York: Random House, 1960, and such texts of the 1970s as M. Angulu Onwuejeogwu. *The Social Anthropology of Africa: An Introduction*. London: Heinemann, 1975; Elliott P. Skinner, ed. *Peoples and Cultures of Africa*. Garden City, N.Y.: Doubleday, 1973; and Colin M. Turnbull, ed. *Africa and Change*. New York: Knopf, 1973.

[12] Melville J. Herskovits. *The Human Factor in Changing Africa*. New York: Knopf, 1962, briefly mentions these topics. In a more specialized study, *Literacy in Traditional Societies*, London: Cambridge, 1968, Jack Goody goes into more detail about the first topic. As the title of Goody's book implies, his interest is in the acquisition of literacy and not in literature per se. However, he does discuss the different meanings of the acquisition of literacy in religious contexts in Ghana, Malagasy, Nigeria, and Somalia, which have influence on the subsequent use of literacy for reading creative writing.

the last generation of Africanist anthropologists in emphasizing the importance of the arts in both ethnic and national African cultures.

John Middleton's *Black Africa* is the only leading introductory text on Africa prepared by an anthropologist used in the 1970s that includes some information on written literature.[13] In the final section "Modernization, Nationalism and Negritude,": two of the five essays are about written literature. One is about negritude by Abiola Irele, who is not an anthropologist, and focuses on the themes of negritude as they express the African response to western contact. The other is about literary sources for studying culture contact by Austin Shelton, an anthropologist, which focuses on the content of four volumes of West African fiction that deal with the theme of a person caught between two cultures. As in the introductory anthropology test on literature, no attention is given to the aesthetic aspects of literature. In fact, this text does not even have a section on the African arts.

Clearly an anthropologist interested in teaching about African literature has few models to follow except those which regard literature as a supplementary source of ethnographic data or those which are provided by folklorists. The latter usually focus on content analyses, although recently some folklorists have given attention to performance and the cultural context of oral literature.[14] Anthropologists have completely ignored literary criticism, although I have outlined an approach to the criticism of African literature from an anthropological perspective.[15]

The challenge to an anthropologist interested in written literature as a cultural phenomenon is to develop teaching strategies for incorporating literature in courses which focus on other subject matter. I have used African literature in the following cultural anthropology courses: Peoples of Subsaharan Africa, Culture Change in Africa, African Political Systems, Introduction to Cultural Anthropology, Cultural Change, Comparative Social Systems, World Ethnography, Anthropology and Education, and Socialization. I also have used literature written by non-Africans, oral literature, and ethnographic fiction written by anthropologists in some of these courses.[16]

There are many reasons for including literature in anthropology courses. Like

---

[13] John Middleton, ed. *Black Africa, Its Peoples and Their Cultures Today.* New York: Macmillan, 1970.

[14] The general outlines of the folklorist approach that I presented in my dissertation, *An Anthropological Analysis of Nigerian Fiction.* Evanston: Northwestern, 1965, are still applicable. Three volumes of papers from the Ninth International Congress of Anthropological and Ethnological Sciences are representative of the current state of the art. *Patterns in Oral Literature*, The Hague: Mouton, 1977, edited by Heda Jason and Demitri Segal, includes thematic and structural analyses that totally divorce oral literature from its cultural contexts and ignore its aesthetic and creative aspects. *Varia Folklorica.* The Hague: Mouton, 1978, edited by Alan Dundes, also includes structural and thematic analyses, which draw more on cultural context than the essays in the preceding volume, but which ignore the creative and aesthetic aspects of the folklore. *Folklore in the Modern World.* The Hague: Mouton, 1978, edited by Richard M. Dorson, is the only volume that contains essays which place folklore in its contemporary cultural contexts. However, the aesthetic aspects of folklore are not covered in these essays.

[15] Nancy J. Schmidt. "Anthropological Criticisms of African Literature." *Ba Shiru* 7, 2 (1976), 1-9.

[16] The only course that I have taught on African literature in over a dozen years of collegiate teaching was an African Studies course rather than an anthropology course. It provided opportunities for using techniques other than those described in this paper.

other anthropologists I recognize that some works of literature provide a more vivid description of limited aspects of culture than do some ethnographies, especially those written by British social anthropologists and those written before the last decade or so when American anthropologists became aware of the cultural gaps in many ethnographies. When carefully presented, literature can be used as a supplement to ethnography to round out descriptions of human behavior. As a humanistic anthropologist, I am interested in all of the arts, or "expressive culture" in the terms of some anthropologists, as both an integral part of a society's culture, and as a vehicle for conveying the meanings of culture in concrete ways as structured and presented by members of the society. Thus I include art, film, music, and oral literature in the same courses in which I include written literature.

In teaching any anthropology course I emphasize the methods used to collect data, the theoretical perspectives that were used to analyze data, and the general validity of the data. I consider this approach essential in teaching anthropology, or any other social sciences, since each social science approaches human behavior in a different way, describes different "facts," and reveals different aspects of the "truth" about human behavior. I also use this kind of approach because it helps teach a basic skill in critical evaluation that can be applied not only in handling social science data in educational contexts, but also in resolving data conflicts outside the formal education system. Thus, every course that I teach is a course about methodology and about a specific topical subdivision of anthropology, and incorporates "expressive culture" more than the average course in cultural anthropology.

Within this general context, I find it easy to teach about literature as an aspect of "expressive culture," as an integral part of a whole culture, and as a reflector of selected facts of behavior. Both literature and ethnography include selective descriptions of culture, each of which must be evaluated on its own terms. These descriptions vary in breadth and depth, for just as there are novels and short stories in literature, so there are monographs and articles in ethnography. These descriptions also vary in their generality and specificity, for just as there are ideological and descriptive novels, so there are ethnographies that focus differentially on cultural values or major cultural themes and on details of social life and material culture. These different types of descriptions may be used alone or in combination, both within a discipline and interdisciplinarily, and must be evaluated accordingly as they are presented in a course.

On a general level, I treat works of literature in the same way as ethnographic reports. I examine them in terms of the personal background of the author or ethnographer, his or her purpose in writing or making an ethnographic study, his or her philosophy of writing or theoretical framework for organizing data, and the audience for whom he or she writes. In other words, I go into considerable detail placing works of literature and ethnography in the cultural contexts of their creation, both as a means to help students gain a better understanding of them when they read them, and as background for discussing selected aspects of their content in class.

Obviously, this type of case study approach limits the number of works of literature that can be considered for inclusion in a course to those of some of the older and more prolific African authors, for a substantial amount of information must be available on an author's personal and literary background if he or she is to be treated like an anthropologist or an anthropologist's informant within the framework of a course.[17] However, many ethnographies also must be excluded from a course syllabus because insufficient background data is available for evaluating their content.[18]

On a specific level, I treat works of literature and ethnography on their own terms in relation to other works of literature and ethnography, as well as in relation to the topic of the course. The specific use of literature and ethnography within each course will vary both with the topic of the course and the specific authors whose works are used as case studies.

To try to make these rather abstract statements more meaningful, I will outline some of the topics covered and works of literature and ethnography discussed in a course on Culture Change in Africa.

Since African literature comprises only a small segment of the data included in an anthropology course, there will be more general discussion that is indirectly related to literature, than there is in a literature course. In a course on culture change, or any other facet of cultural anthropology, this information will include background for the works of literature used in case studies, even though this is not the explicit purpose for including the material in the course. For example, in a course on culture change in Africa, literature will be discussed in the context of educational change, both in terms of the acquisition of literacy, curriculum goals, literature read, and literature written for schoolchildren. Literature also will be included in discussing the development of nationalism as it pertains to Africaniza-tion following the colonial era, and the development of nationalism as it pertains to Africanization following the colonial era, and the development of national pride through emphasis on national culture. Literature again will be discussed in relation to the mass media and publishing, both of which are related to the development of nationalism, as well as to other sociocultural factors that are considered in the course.

One case study in the course on changes in village life will include works of literature and ethnography. The Igbo of Nigeria are the focus of the case study, for which three books are assigned:[19] *Things Fall Apart* by Chinua Achebe, *Igbo Village Affairs* by Margaret Green, and *Igbo of Southeastern Nigeria* by Victor Uchendu.[20] The personal background of each author and content of his or her work are discussed in relation to other topics covered in the course, as well as being

[17] It is works by the same group of authors that are readily availabe in paperback in the U.S.A.

[18] It is only within the last two decades that some anthropologists have become aware of the need for systematically providing background about how ethnographic studies are made, and are willing to openly discuss both strengths and weaknesses of their own fieldwork. This change has coincided with the rapid expansion of anthropology as an undergraduate course of study, among other factors.

[19] Usually I use only one ethnography and one novel in a case study, but I chose this atypical example to more clearly demonstrate the potentials of the kind of case study method that I use.

[20] Chinua Achebe. *Things Fall Apart*. London: Heinemann, 1958; M.M. Green. *Igbo Village Affairs*. New York: Praeger, 1964 (c1947); Victor C. Uchendu. *The Igbo of Southeastern Nigeria*. New York: Holt, Rinehart and Winston, 1965.

compared to each other. I will provide only a few examples for each author, since time precludes presenting a complete outline of how these works are integrated into the course.

Margaret Green was a British social anthropologist who made her study of the Igbo between 1934 and 1937, while she was employed by the colonial government in Nigeria. Her study and its methodology can easily be related to principles of colonial administration and the role that anthropologists had in British colonial Africa. The theoretical framework that she used for her study, that emphasized psychological differences between the Igbo and British, was based on the work of Murdo Mackenzie.[21] This framework also influenced British colonial administrators, since it was part of the general intellectual background of educated Britons at that time. Green's study was conducted, in part, as an attempt to gain a better understanding of the Igbo following the Aba Riots of 1929-1930. Its topical emphasis on law and women's organization, which occupies nine of the fifteen chapters, was influenced by this historical coincidence, rather than by facets of culture of major concern to the Igbo. Green's description of Igbo village life is that of an outsider who is unable to identify with the people, and her framework for presenting data is that of her own culture.

Victor Uchendu is an Igbo and one of the first generation of Nigerian-trained anthropologists, who conducted a study of his own culture in the early 1960s. Since he was born at approximately the time that Green made her study, the sociocultural context of his study and the details of village life available for description provide a marked contrast to those at the time that Green made her study. Uchendu's study and its methodology can easily be related to the development of formal education in Nigeria and the roles assumed by the first generation of the Ibadan-educated elite. The theoretical framework that he uses is that of British social anthropology, but it is from a later generation than Green's, and is related to an intellectual climate of nationalism in Nigeria and cultural relativism in anthropology. The intended audience of Uchendu's study is American college undergraduates, rather than British colonial officials and other Britons curious about Africa, as was Green's, although Uchendu collected his data for a research project sponsored by Ibadan University.[22] Uchendu's topical coverage of village life is broader and more balanced than Green's, and Igbo values, frequently expressed in proverbs, are given prominence in the presentation of the data. Uchendu's description of Igbo village life is that of a sympathetic, but emotionally detached insider, whose framework for presenting data is that of mid-twentieth

[21] Murdo Mackenzie. *The Human Mind*. London: Churchill, 1940 and *When Temperaments Clash*. London: Murby, 1937.

[22] Uchendu's residence in the U.S.A. and his professional contacts at Northwestern University where he was engaged in doctoral studies account for his writing an ethnography for American undergraduates. There was no market for undergraduate texts in anthropology in Nigeria at the time that Uchendu wrote this ethnography. The editors of the Case Studies in Anthropology Series were especially interested in publishing Uchendu's ethnography because of its atypical anthropological status: "This case study is one of those rare events in anthropological literature — an ethnography written by one of the people whose culture is being described." Uchendu, *The Igbo*, p. vii.

century social anthropology.[23]

Chinua Achebe is an Igbo and one of Nigeria's best known creative writers. Like Uchendu, he is one of the first generation of Ibadan-trained Nigerians, but his course of study and professional contacts were different from Uchendu's. Achebe's writing career and his goals in writing fiction can easily be related to the development of Nigerian nationalism, the Africanization of the mass media and school curricula after Nigerian independence, the development of local publishing in Nigeria, the growth of Nigerian creative writing in the post-Word War II period, and the internationalization of African literature.[24] The same intellectual climate influences both Achebe's and Uchendu's writing, but their fields of scholarly interest and places of primary residence (Nigeria and the U.S.A.), result in their expressing this shared heritage in different ways. The intended audience of Achebe's fiction is both Nigerian and international.[25] The topical coverage of his village fiction is more historical, religious and personal (in the sense of focusing on individual personalities) than is that of Green's and Uchendu's ethnographies. Igbo values permeate Achebe's village fiction and are frequently presented in proverbs and English renditions of Igbo idioms of speech.[26] Achebe's descriptions of Igbo village life are those of a sensitive, emotionally involved insider, who uses the techniques of Igbo oral tradition, to tell a story within which details of selected aspects of village life are embedded.

I hope that these three capsule summaries have suggested the great potential for comparing these three works of ethnography and literature in a course on culture change in Africa. The content of the three works is discussed in relation to the kinds of background factors that I have just outlined. Each book explicitly deals with Igbo culture change and collectively the three books deal with changes in eastern Nigeria from the precolonial period until the present, so that they include far more data than can be analyzed in detail in one case study. However, the course includes other case studies, and students write papers based on ethnographies and novels that are not assigned in the course, which provide opportunities for extending the kinds of comparisons that are made in one case study.

By using the teaching strategies that I have all-too-briefly outlined in this paper, it is hoped that students will gain an appreciation for both African literature and African ethnography, rather than viewing African literature only as a supplementary source of ethnographic data on culture change or other facets of African culture.[27]

[23] Differences between British social anthropology and American cultural anthropology are discussed in the course, especially because social anthropologists do not give systematic attention to expressive culture. These differences also must be discussed as background for comparing ethnographies of African communities written by British and American anthropologists.

[24] It is in connection with the latter two topics that background on criticism of African literature is brought into the course.

[25] The unintended audience of his fiction, such as secondary schoolchildren in English-speaking nations where his writing has been translated, are discussed in the course.

[26] Presenting idioms in this way is quite different from the approach taken by anthropologists, including both Uchendu and Green, in which the Igbo words are used and either a literal translation or explanation of their derivation is provided.

[27] If there were more time, I could outline how I use films, African art, and oral literature in providing information relevant to gaining an appreciation of African written literature.

THE WEST INDIAN PRESENCE IN THE WORKS OF THREE NEW CENTRAL AMERICAN WRITERS

Ian I. Smart

Howard University

Introduction

> Where then is the nigger's home?
> In Paris Brixton Kingston Rome?
>
> Edward Brathwaite, *Rights of Passage*.

A seemingly interminable cycle of wanderings and migrations has been the destiny of many African peoples for countless centuries. The relocation of thousands upon thousands of African people from the English-speaking islands of the Caribbean to Spanish-speaking lands of Central America is just one more episode in this history of "Scatteration". The tide began flowing to Panama in the 1850s, followed by two more great waves in the 1880s and the first decade of this century. The most significant wave of migration to Costa Rica dates back to the 1870s.[1] It took three generations of sweat and sorrow for these Anglophone Caribbean Africans to realize that there was no turning back. When the third generation became literate in Spanish, a new kind of Panamanian and Costa Rican (among others) literature was born. This is a literature that in many ways reflects the Anglophone West Indian heritage of about 10% of the Panamanian population[2] and 2% of Costa Rica's.[3]

Because the first two generations of Anglophone West Indians clung steadfast-

---

[1] This factual information can be gleaned from many sources. My immediate sources were: Melva Low Ocran, "El idioma inglés y la integración social de los panameños de origen afro-antillano al carácter nacional." *Revista Nacional de Cultura*, No. 5 (Oct. Nov. Dic. 1976), p. 25. For the Costa Rican data I used: Carlos Meléndez and Quince Duncan, *El negro en Costa Rica* (San José: Editorial Costa Rica, 1978), p. 65.

It is of interest to know that Marcus Garvey himself was once part of this tide of immigrants. So too was Joseph N. Hibbert, one of the founders of the Rastafarian Movement. He "...was born in 1894. At age 17 he migrated to Costa Rica where he lived for 20." (Leonard Barrett, *The Rastafarians*. Boston: Beacon, 1977, p. 82).

[2] Preston E. James, *Latin America* (New York: Odyssey Press, 1942), gives the following population breakdown: 67% Mestizo or Mulatto, 11% Caucasoid, 6% Indian, 1% East Indian, Chinese etc., and 15% Black — mostly of Anglophone Caribbean background (p. 208). The *Area Handbook of Panama*, (Washington, D.C.: U.S. Government Printing, 1972), 98, gives a slightly different version; the variation presumably being a consequence of updating: 70% Mestizo, Mulatto, 10% White, 13% Black (8% being "West Indian," 5% being "*negros coloniales*"), the Indians and Orientals remain constant. In the matter of the ethnic breakdown of a population the figures tend to reflect as much the compiler's point of view as the actual reality. Hence I feel that the 10% figure I have used is a fair estimate.

[3] See Meléndez and Duncan, p. 87.

ly to the traditions imposed on them by a cleverly designed British colonizing machine, their experience with literature was exclusively a hand-me-down, servile relationship with the British classics: Shakespeare, Sir Walter Scott, Mrs. H.B. Stowe, Tennyson, to name but a few of the more important authors.[4] It was during the 1940s when the Anglophone West Indian population was approximately beginning its third generation in exile that its first important Spanish-language literary figures were born: Quince Duncan (1940) in the province of Limón, Costa Rica; Carlos Guillermo Wilson (1941), and Gerardo Maloney (1944), both in Panama. Duncan and Maloney have remained in their native countries; the former indeed has already gained national and international recognition. He now resides in San José, the national capital, where he earns his living as a college professor and to some extent from his writings as historian, essayist, short story writer, and novelist. His published books to date number seven.[5] Maloney is still very much a new poet. He lives in Panama City, but his reputation is still confined to a small circle of "knowledgeable" intellectuals both inside and outside of Panama.[6] He is a college professor of sociology, and he is also very involved in community organizations. Carlos G. Wilson, who prefers to be called by his pen name, Cubena, has extended the "scatteration" process to the United States — like so many Central Americans of Anglophone West Indian background. Even in the United States Cubena cannot make a living as a writer, so he too is a college professor — of Spanish — at Loyola Marymount University in Los Angeles, California. He has published two small volumes to date: one of poetry, the other of short stories. He recently completed the writing of his first novel, *Chombo*.[7]

In every respect the biographies of these men tell the tale of an essential West Indian experience, a cycle of migration and readaptation. However, they, like some of their Central American compatriots represent a special breed of West Indians whose destiny has made them fully pan-Caribbean; they are bilingual and bicultural in two of the important languages and cultures that contribute to the Caribbean melting pot. They are people who speak an English that to an untrained listener is totally Jamaican, who sing calypsoes, enjoy Carnival, give "picong,"[8]

---

[4] Ibid., p. 127.

[5] The two works by Duncan not mentioned in the course of this paper are: *Los cuatro espejos* (San José: Editorial Costa Rica, 1973) — a novel — and *El negro en la literatura costarricense* (San José, Editorial Costa Rica, 1975). The former is no longer in print. For more information on Duncan the reader may wish to refer to, Richard L. Jackson, *Black Writers in Latin America* (Albuquerque: University of New Mexico Press, 1979), pp. 18, 47-48, 127-129.

[6] Maloney has been promising a book of poems for at least two years now. As of summer 1980 it had not been published.

[7] *Chombo* as of August 1980 had still not been published. His book of poems, entitled *Pensamientos del negro Cubena* (Los Angeles, 1977), is not mentioned in the course of this paper. For more information on Cubena the reader may see the book by Jackson, already mentioned (above, note 5), or an article of mine: Ian I. Smart, "Big Rage Rage and Big Romance: Discovering a New Panamanian Author," *Caribbean Review*, 8, No. 3 (1979), 34-38.

[8] "Picong" is a Trinidadian Creole terms used to describe a kind of humour that is almost a way of life with Trinidadians. To "give picong" is to poke fun at the foibles of relatives, friends, acquaintances, public figures, eliciting the warm laughter of the community and frequently of the person who is the butt of the jokes. Much of this humour is based on verbal virtuosity of all kinds. "Picong" is central to the calypso art form. It is analogous to the other types of satirical humour that are popular among many African peoples, both of the continent and in the "Scatteration."

and identify with relatives and friends in Jamaica, Barbados, Trinidad, etc., but who have produced a literature written in Spanish. Such a literature is as much Hispanic and Latin American as it is Caribbean and West Indian. Our paper will examine the Anglophone West Indian presence in this literature, focussing on two areas in which this presence is most clearly evidenced: language and religion.

Language

On the basis of their respective linguistic background, Panamanian, Costa Rican, and other Central American societies establish a definite cleavage in their African population groups. On the one hand there are those whose whole language is Spanish, and who can trace their roots back to the colonial period (the sixteenth to the nineteenth centuries). These are the "colonial blacks" — *negros coloniales*. On the other hand there are those whose Anglophone West Indian background combines with their blackness to stamp them indelibly as "*chombos*," "*chumecas*," *jamaiquinos*,[9] to mention some of the more frequently used and less than polite appellations. The English surname serves as the most important identifying feature of this latter group. This English surname quite commonly combines with a Hispanic first name, as in the cases of Gerardo Maloney, and Carlos Wilson. Quince Duncan's case where both names are English, is, nowadays, the exception rather than the rule — particularly in Panama. The presence of the so-called "*chombos*"[10] afford the "colonial blacks" some relief from the full burden of the systematic and repugnant racism that is practised in Panama, Costa Rica, and indeed in all parts of Central, South and North America. For linguistic

---

[9] The reader should bear in mind that similar groups of black folks of Anglophone Caribbean background exist in Nicaragua — mostly in Bluefields — in Belize, obviously, and even in Venezuela, Cuba, the Dominican Republic and Puerto Rico. In the last two countries they are called among other names, *cocolos*.

[10] It is imperative at this point to make some clarifications with regard to the terms that will be used in this paper. The matter of these terms used to describe the various population groups in Panama and Costa Rica is very complex and indeed most delicate. However, in a paper of this sort the use of some of these terms cannot be avoided. It should be noted first and foremost that "*chumeca*" and "*chombo*" are terms of abuse. However, I have noticed a tendency on the part of some of my Panamanian friends and in-laws to neutralize the venom of the term "*chombo*" by using it proudly, defiantly, and lovingly to describe themselves. This process is exactly analogous to that by which "nigger" has been purged of its vicious insulting nature in the view of some younger and militant Black North Americans. The term "*chumeca*," still seems to be utterly unacceptable.

In my view the more polite designations, Afro-Antillean Panamanian, *Afro-panameño antillano*, West Indian, or *antillano* are inadequate since the suggest that the other population groups are not Antillean or Caribbean. This implication would be inaccurate in the case of Panama at least, for it can be reasonably argued that Panama is a Caribbean country — or at least a circum-Caribbean country. In the case of Costa Rica, the terms: *antillano*, West Indian, Afro-Antillean Costa Rican would be acceptable. The term *criollo* (Creole) has been used to describe Panamanians and Costa Ricans of Anglophone Caribbean background, but I prefer to avoid it since "Creole" means so many entirely different things throughout the Americas and even in Africa. The most accurate umbrella term is, in my view, Central Americans of Anglophone Caribbean background. This is somewhat cumbersome, so, at times, for the sake of avoiding complicated wording I will make use of the less accurate but polite designation "West Indian."

I will use the term *latinos* in this paper to refer to those Panamanians and Costa Ricans whose linguistic background is exclusively Hispanic. These may be either *negros coloniales* or "paña," "Spanish" — "paña" or "Spanish" are terms used by Central Americans of Anglophone Caribbean background to describe *latinos* who are either white or *mestizo*.

background has become the most important determinant of ethnicity, and thus Hispanicity of the "colonial blacks" tends to outweigh their blackness. Only the blacks of Anglophone Caribbean background are considered "niggers" in the thoroughly negative sense of this term.

Even though the second generation Central Americans of Anglophone Caribbean background inherited their parents' disdain for the Spanish language and shared their dream of returning home to the islands, they began to make an effort to learn Spanish. Their peculiar linguistic situation provided artistic possibilities which were first developed by *latino* authors from Panama and Costa Rica. Carlos Luis Fallas in his novel, *Mamita Yunai* (1950), and the Panamanian Joaquín Beleño C., in *Gamboa Road Gang* (1960), to mention some outstanding examples. These sympathetic "non-West-Indian" authors used the defective Spanish of their "West Indian" characters to heighten the pathos of their dismal socioeconomic situation. Tom Winkelman, one of the minor characters in *Puerto Limón* is a case in point. The following sample of his Spanish displays some of the characteristic linguistic flaws of the second generation Central American of Anglophone Caribbean background:

> — Ruby? Ruby morir hace tres años. Entonces yo trabajar de jardinero y Ruby de cocinera donde Míster Maker, el superintendente de la Compañía. — Al hablar de su esposa la alegría, que le había iluminado el rostro al ver el mar, desapareció. — Ruby se enferma y no la cuidaron — añadió con voz baja. — Nosotros trabajar con ellos, quince años trabajar con ellos, y no la cuidaron. Yo hacer de todo.[11]
>
> ("Ruby? Ruby die three years ago. Then I work as gardener and Ruby as cook by Mister Maker, the Company superintendent." As he spoke about his wife the joy, that had lighted up his face on seeing the sea, disappeared. "Ruby get sick and they didn't look after her," he added in a low voice. "We work with them, fifteen years work with them, and they didn't look after her. I do everything.")

Tom's most obvious problem is with the verb paradigm. He frequently substitutes the infinitive for the appropriate inflected form of the verb. His grammatical impotence, in counterpoint to the implied author's impeccable prose, adequately matches his utter helplessness in the socioeconomic order.

By the third generation — to speak generally, with some degree of oversimplification that generalities always demand — the days of "Tarzan talk" were over, although some of the grosser traces of "Anglophonism" did remain in the speech of some "West Indians." For example. the white *latino* of the main character in Duncan's *Los cuatro espejos* recalls her contact with a black schoolmate and describes him as: "...a timid, bad-tempered boy who pronoucned his 'h's' and dropped his 'j's'.[12] This particular young man, if he existed in the real world,

---

[11] *Puerto Limón* (San José: Editorial Costa Rica, 1970), p. 46.

[12] *Los cuatro espejos* (San José: Editorial Costa Rica, 1973), p. 127: "...un muchacho tímido, de mal carácter, que pronunciaba sus haches aspiradas y omitía las jotas."
   Throughout the paper I shall translate all the Spanish quotes unless (as was the case with the quote corresponding to note 11) the original Spanish is necessary in order to make the point. In the interest of scholarship, I will put the original Spanish in the notes.

would have been a contemporary of Quince Duncan, but he retained one of the more obvious characteristics of Jamaican speech. This feature conflicts sharply with an important rule of Spanish orthography: the English "h" sound is symbolized in writing by a "j" or "g"; never by an "h".

Although it can be said that in general Central Americans of Anglophone Caribbean background of the third and later generations are native speakers of Spanish, they continue to be victims of a discrimination based not only on race but on linguistic background. This general problem is given dramatic expression in a scene from *Los cuatro espejos*. The protagonist, Charles McForbes, overhears a conversation on a bus between two Costa Ricans, one *latino* the other "West Indian." The *latino* after a while asks his black interlocutor if he is Panamanian. The conversation then continues:

> "No, why?"
> "You speak Spanish very well."
> "I'm from Limón," he said, smiling.[13]

The *latino* assumes that all black people who speak Spanish must belong to the "colonial black" group. Because there are relatively few of this group in Costa Rica, the *latino* concludes that his interlocutor must be from the neighboring country of Panama, where much of the population belongs to the "colonial black" category. The protagonist, however, immediately grasps all the odious racist implications of the *latino's* apparently innocent question, and unmasks them in the following comments he makes to himself:

> I would not have smiled at him. The guy had made one of those sweeping logical deductions: everyone from Limón, by virtue of his or her West Indian heritage, speaks Spanish badly. The lecturer's world came back to me and the whole business infuriated me. "If a *latino* uses the wrong gender, everybody understands that it was just a slip of the tongue. If a black person commits the same fault everybody who hears him will smile ironically."
> Damn, I could have socked the guy for saying that.[14]

Linguistic indicators of Anglophone Caribbean heritage are, then, of tremendous sociological as well as artistic significance. In the emerging literature created by the new Central Americans of Anglophone Caribbean background these indicators have the important function of bearing testimony to the "West Indianness" of this literature. In the first instance, the very names of the fictional characters bear testimony to their Anglophone Caribbean heritage. Charles McForbes is the main character in Duncan's *Los cuatro espejos*, and Lorena Sam, daughter of Mr. Sam the obeahman, is the only woman he ever truly loves. Some

---

[13] — No, por qué?
  — Habla muy bien el español.
  — Soy limonense — dijo sonriendo (p. 20).

[14] Yo no le hubiera sonreído. El tipo había hecho una de esas grandes deducciones lógicas: todo limonense, por ser de herencia antillana, habla mal el español. Las palabras del conferencista regresaron a mis oídos y eso me dio mucha rabia. "Si une persona latina emplea mal el género, la audiencia comprende que fue un error sin importancia. Si un negro comete la misma falta, provocará la sonrisa irónica del público."
  Carajo, le hibiera podido muy bien dar un buen puñetazo al tipo que dijo eso (p. 20.)

of the minor characters, all from the province of Limón, are Ruth, Jakel Duke, Clif Brown, and Alfred George. In *La paz del pueblo*, Duncan's latest novel published in 1978, the main characters are Sitaira Kenton, Pedro Dull and Cató Brown. José Gordon is the protagonist of an important short story, "La leyenda de Josée Gordon," from the collection, *La rebelión pocomía* (1976). In one of his poems, "Testimonios" (to be discussed later), Maloney evokes the West Indian world by simply mentioning names like Rupert, Grace, Ginger, and Robert. Both of Cubena's books are dedicated to Papa James and Nenén (the Hispanic form of "Nen-nen", a term of respect and endearment used in the Anglophone Caribbean to refer to the grandmother or godmother or simply an older woman.

Papa James and Nen-nen appear as characters in the story, "Luna de miel." There they are a benevolent West Indian couple, well-known for their uncommon generosity. Nen-nen at one time in her life earned a living selling: "...chicheme, bollos, carimañolas, bakes, souce, sopa de guandú, empanadas, pescado frito, ceviche sancocho, guacho."[15] This list of typical foods eaten at wayside stalls and cafes in Panama City aptly reflects the Anglophone Caribbean heritage. The words "bake" and "souce" retain their original English form, however, the "patty"[16] has been rechristened with the eminently Hispanic form, *"empanada;"* *"ceviche"* is really the author's way of designating "escoveitched;" and *"sancocho"* is also a Spanish rendering of a popular culinary term from the Anglophone Caribbean. The exclamations, "cho," of obvious Jamaican provenience, and "hey" are frequently used by Duncan's and Cubena's characters. In fact, the aspiration of the "h" in "hey" defies the general practice of Hispanic phonology. More consistent with the laws of Spanish morphology is Duncan's use of the form *"obeahmanes"* as the plural of "obeahman."[17]

The *latino* authors in general use the peculiarities of speech of their "West Indian" characters for local color effect and to attempt to make such characters more authentic. Duncan's Cubena's, and Maloney's use of these linguistic phe-

---

[15] *Cuentos del negro Cubena* (Guatemala: Editorial Landívar, 1977), p. 34.

[16] A patty is a kind of meat pie that is very popular in Jamaica or wherever Jamaicans have settled.
   "Escoveitched" refers to a special way of preparing fish that is popular with Jamaicans at home and abroad.
   For many West Indians from the islands the term "sankotch" (this spelling is the one that to my mind most accurately reflects the pronunciation that I am familiar with) refers to a style of preparing food. According to this style different food stuffs are mixed together and "cooked up" to make one dish.

[17] An obeahman is one who engages in obeah. The term obeah is used widely throughout the entire Caribbean, and needs no explanation to most Caribbean and even non-Caribbean readers. However, for the sake of scholarly integrity, I shall offer Duncan's explanation of obeah and obeahman given in the glossary to *La paz del pueblo*: "Obeah: poder. Obeahman: hombre de poder. Brujo que utiliza su poder para bien o para mal...." (Obeah: power. Obeahman: a man with the power. A conjurer who uses his power for good or for evil....) The glossary to Claude McKay's *Banana Bottom* (New York, 1933) describes Obeah as a "West Indian form of African magic." The process applied here is akin to the one by which "girl," prounounced "gal," becomes *"galcita,"* and "boy," pronounced "buoy," becomes *"buoycito"* (*cito,* and *cita* are diminutive suffixes in Spanish). The latter process is itself quite active in the grammar of present-day "West Indian" blacks from Panama who are native speakers of Spanish. Indeed, all of the words discussed above and analogous forms like: *"fren"* and *"frenita"* (from "friend"), or *"bróder"* (from "brother"), or *"mista"* (from "Mister"), are fast becoming part of the language of all urban Panamanians, *latinos* as well as those of Anglophone Caribbean background.

nomena achieves a similar effect. However, their handling of the phenomena has, in addition, resulted in a real enrichment of the Spanish lexicon. For the frequent traces of their Anglophone West Indian background found in their Spanish are not mere jarring intrusions of a foreign and essentially incompatible phonological system. Rather, the evidence the existence of the trend towards the harmonious incorporation of "West Indian" elements into the Spanish of contemporary Central Americans.[18] Maloney, moreover, has attempted a more daring experiement with the linguistic peculiarities created by the presence of Panamanians of Anglophone Caribbean background; he has incorporated into them the very structure of one of his works.

The poem in question is "Testimonios," one of the four published in Panama's prestigious *Revista Nacional de Cultura* (No. 5, Oct. Nov. Dec. 1976). It presents for the reader's consideration two of the basic elements that compose that nation's reality. These are the culture and world of the Panamanians of Anglophone Caribbean background, and the culture and world of the *latinos*. The first half of the poem treats the "West Indians," so that the opening stanza begins with one line in Spanish with the next six in Panamanian English and concludes with four more lines in Spanish:

> Aquí está el Testimonio... (Here is the Testimony)
> — Granny
> Notin in the pat to eat
> son
> No money again today
> The Lord with provide
> Some day. —
> Aquí Yace Winfred Smallhorne
> Descanse en paz,
> y en la Memoria de sus seres queridos
> en las constancias de la marcha Subterránea.
>
> (Here Lies Winfred Smallhorne
> May he rest in peace,
> and in the Memory of his loved ones
> in all the immutability of the journey
> through Hades.)

Reflecting the pronunciation of Panamanian English — a language very similar to Jamaican English — "nothing" is written as *notin*, and "pot" becomes *pat*. Further on in the work *Jahn* is used for "John," and *Winstan* for "Winston" without any need for authorial comment. The switching from Spanish to English and back again is a feature of the speech of many bilingual, bicultural black people from Panama and Costa Rica. Its use in this poem represents a serious attempt to tap the aesthetic potential of the phenomenon.

The preceding pages presented some reflections on the vital significance of

---

[18] In fact, a recent novel, *Loma ardiente y vestida de sol* (Panama: Ediciones INAC, 1977) by the young *latino* Panamanian Fafael L. Pernett y Morales (born 1949) provides many examples of the Anglophone Caribbean influence on Panamanian Spanish.

their Anglophone background in the life and letters of the "West Indian" population groups in Panama and Costa Rica. Important as it is, language is obviously
just one facet of the culture of these Central Americans of Anglophone Caribbean
background. Religion is another extremely important aspect of this culture.

Religion

Edward Brathwaite, in his article, "The African Presence in Caribbean Literature," (*Daedalus*, 103, No. 2, 1974, 73-109), makes the point that African culture
is religious centered, so that: "...It is therefore not surprising that anthropologists
tell us that African culture survived in the Caribbean through religion" (p. 74).
Duncan's fictional universe reflects the real life distinction between the world of
the *latinos* and that of the Central Americans of Anglophone Caribbean background. The linguistic features already viewed serve to delineate the world of the
latter. So too, then, must the question of religion. In almost all of Duncan's short
stories set among the "West Indian" people, the religious theme occupies a
central position. In his two latest novels, *Los cuatro espejos* (1973), and *La paz del
pueblo* (1978), the theme is also of pivotal significance. The idea of conflict
between the West Indian's "magical" interpretation of reality and the so-called
"scientific" approach of the *latino* (white/*mestizo*) establishment is naturally of
particular interest to Duncan the artist. The syncretism of elements from the
established *latino* religion, Catholicism, or the established Jamaican Anglican-
ism, with elements of African religions is also an important artistic stimulus for
Duncan.

"La luz del vigía," from Duncan's first book, *Una canción en la nadrugada*
(San José, 1970), is a rather humorous short story telling the tale of the mysterious
antics of what appears to be a ghostly signal light (luz) in the equally ghostly hands
of a brakeman (vigía), who met his death in an unfortunate accident. A skeptical
group of young village boys decides to probe the mystery and they are chastened
by the disturbingly inexplicable antics of the ghostly light. Their elementary
school teacher discovers what transpired and scoffs at their backwardness as she
champions the cause of "science." She declares: "I have fought against supersti-
tion in the classroom; this would be a great opportunity to do so now in the very
place where these imaginary things supposedly took place," [19] She too is forced
ultimately to yield to the power of the mystery after a sobering encounter with the
ghostly light. It would be impossible to find a person who has grown up in the
Caribbean islands who does not have a similar tale to tell, either from hearsay or
from his own experience.

In another short story, "La rebelión pocomía, "which gives the title to
Duncan's second collection of short stories (1976), Jean Paul is possessed by

---

[19] "He luchado contra la superstición en las lecciones, valga la oportunidad de hacerlo en el propio
escenario de los hechos imaginados por ustedes" (p. 54).

"*cuminá*"[20] and thereby given the strength to lead the struggle against oppression and exploitation. The motif of possession by an African "god" is frequently found in Caribbean literature. One such example is the case of Dieudonné in *All Men are Mad*, a novel by the Haitians Phillipe Thoby-Marcelin and his brother Pierre Marcelin. Dieudonné is a frail fifteen-year-old boy who is possessed by Ogou Ferraille, the "god" of war, and is turned into a raging warrior with tragicomic consequences for the youth.[21] The symbolic link between African religious phenomena and political action is particularly pertinent to the Caribbean experience. Professor Barrett (in the work already referred to) points out, for example, that the Sam Sharpe Rebellion, the Morant Bay Rebellion, and the Rastafarian Movement were all inspired by the African-based religiosity of Jamaican folk. Many commentators, including C.L.R. James and Jean Price-Mars,[22] contend that the Voodoo religion of the Haitian masses provided the essential organizational base for the successful armed revolt that led to Haitian independence in 1804. Furthermore, *cumíná* (Kumina), and *pocomía* (Pukimina) are central to the religious experience of the Jamaican masses (even allowing for the special Costa Rican understanding of "cuminá").

In *La paz del pueblo* (San José: Editorial Costa Rica, 1978), the character of the rebel inspired by African religion reappears in the person of Pedro Dull, the main male protagonist. Pedro is a thorn in the side of the powers that be, represented by Brown, a rich landowner, and an unnamed establishment clergyman. The latter expressly accuses Pedro of disrupting the peace of the people (la paz del pueblo), declaring from the pulpit in a clearly understood reference to Pedro: "...the peace of this village has been disturbed by persons who are not even from here."[23] However, at the very end of the novel as Pedro's mission assumes definite messianic proportions, the author reaffirms his relationship with *cumíná* (in the

---

[20] Obviously this is the Hispanicized form of Kumina, which Barrett (see note 1) explains thus: "The word comes from two Twi words: *Akom* — "to be possessed," and *Ana* — "by an ancestor." The Jamaicans in Costa Rica developed a somewhat different concept of "kumina" (*cumíná*). Duncan, in his glossary to *La paz de pueblo*, lists "Cuminá" as simply, "dios" (god). This is the same explanation that he gives for "Nyambe" and "Shangó." In Jamaica the name "Kumina" is used to refer firstly to the folk religion of certain Jamaicans whose primary form of ritual is a rite of possession by ancestors. The term Kumina also refers to the ritual celebration itself. In Costa Rica the term has evolved to refer to the power, or "loa," "god," or ancestor who possesses the devotee. Thus *cumíná* has become the same kind of entity as Shango, Ogou Ferraille, Oshun, Yemeyá, and all the other "powers" who possess the members of the various Afro folk religions in the Caribbean. Thus although *cumíná* and "Kumina" ate intimately related, the reader should be aware of the subtle difference between the two terms. The reader should also bear in mind that the term "Kumina" itself has two meanings for Jamaicans.

Pocomía for the Costa Ricans retains the same meaning as Pukumina for the Jamaicans. Barrett describes Pukumina as an Afro-Christian sect tending more toward the traditional African religions than traditional Euro-Christianity (see page 24). This description concurs with Duncan's description of *pocomía* (in *El negro en Costa Rica*, p. 121).

[21] Translation br Eva Thoby-Marcelin (New York: Farrar, Straus & Girous, 1970), see p. 87.

[22] See James's *The Black Jacobins* (New York: Knopf, 1963), especially the first pages of Chapter IV, "The San Domingo Masses Begin." Price Mars' views are reported by Sidney Mintz in his introduction to Alfred Métraux, *Voodoo in Haiti*. Trans. Hugo Charteris (New York: Schocken, 1972), p. 10.

[23] "...la paz de este pueblo ha sido alterada por personas que ni siquiera son de aquí" (p. 149).

Costa Rican sense of a "deity" or *loa*), who, taking possession of Pedro, dances the peace of the people. The message is that peace can only come about as a result of successful resistance to the exploitation and oppression by the white/*mestizo* establishment.

This central message of the novel may yield in importance, for the casual reader, to Pedro's entanglement in a triangular relationship with the maddeningly beautiful Sitaira, a young woman of eccentric ways who has the whole village in a veritable tizzy. Her murder by Cató, Brown's less than well-balanced son, is meant to tie in with the theme of Pedro's mystical call to revolution. The relationship between Sitaira, Cató Brown, and Pedro is built up of torturously interwoven strands that lead back to the histories of their respective ancestors on a plantation in nineteenth-century Jamaica. The author's narrative technique, based on the magical realism and critical realism popular in the contemporary Latin American novel form, confounds the tangle of threads with some readers may probably enjoy unraveling. Furthermore, the world portrayed by Duncan is one ruled by the laws of the *Samamfo* — the Ashanti concept of the state or place in which the spirits of the living dead reside (as Duncan explains in his glossary). A complex and sophisticated work, *La paz del pueblo* provides a most interesting treatment of the African religious heritage in the Caribbean.

The earlier novel, *Los cuatro espejos*, presents the problem of one Charles McForbes, an Afro-Antilean from Limón, who, cast adrift from his moorings in the folk culture, undergoes an extreme identity crisis but resolves his problem finally through a spiritual and physical journey back to his roots. The root of the problem lies in Charles' exposure to the "scientific" world of the white/*mestizo, latino* establishment during the period in which he undertook his secondary studies in the capital. However, the real test came when his first wife, Lorena Sam, herself the daughter of a highly reputed obeahman, Mr. Sam, is attacked by a *dopí*[24] — a "duppy" The "*dopí*," it turns out, was commissioned either by a jilted lover, Cristian Bowman, or by Nabe, his wife, who is fiercely jealous of Lorena. All the sophisticated science of the San José medical establishment proves useless against the "*dopí*," and Lorena dies after a long, expensive, and ultimately inexplicable illness. Her death triggers Charles' abandonment of his community to lose himself completely in the white *latino* world of the capital with the results already mentioned. This novel, like *La paz del pueblo*, continues the Latin American narrative tradition established by works such as *Pedro Páramo*, *La muerte de Artemio Cruz*, and *Cien años de soledad*, to mention but these three. Its plot is quite complex but Lorena's death can be considered the key action of the novel. The author is at pains to point out that this death is the result of obeah too powerful for the "scientific" world to counteract.

The syncretism the reader sees in the West Indian religious world portrayed in Duncan's works provides yet another link with the folk religious tradition in the Caribbean islands.[25] Charles McForbes, for example, was at one time a part-time

[24] Duncan defines "dopí" as, "aparición; espíritu de persona muerta." (Apparition; spirit of a dead person.) This coincides with the popular idea in the rest of the Caribbean that a "duppy" is some sort of ghost or spirit.

[25] The reader interested in this topic should consult works like Métraux's, mentioned in note 22 above.

pastor, having done his secondary studies in some type of seminary (the matter is not explained clearly). However, this pastor unhesitatingly goes to consult Mr. Sam the obeahman, his future father-in-law, when he suspects that the unusually low yield of his small holding may be the result of some praeternatural intervention at the behest of his rival Cristian Bowman. Mr. Sam's prescriptions are themselves a fascinating example of the syncretism of Christianity and the traditional West African religions:

> "Every night you must put a bucket of water in the yard. Then rub down with this and go to bed."...
>
> "You have to get up very early every morning and sprinkle the farm with the water along the side that borders on Cristian's place..."
>
> "And when you get to the farm you must say: 'the Lord is great and strong seven times.'"[26]

The two basic elements of Mr. Sam's recommendations can be considered to be totally rooted in traditional African religiosity. The sprinkling, a form of libation, is quite common to African folk religion practised in the Caribbean (as anyone who has witnessed Shango, Santería, or suchlike ceremonies will agree). The second element, the prayer to the Lord, the One True God ("le Bon Dieu," Olodumare) is equally consonant with African religious tradition. For Africans were the first in human history to organize a monotheistic state religion.[27] However, on the other hand the idea of sprinkling "holy" water, and the invocation repeated a ritual number of times are elements that many would view as eminently, if not peculiarly, Catholic. In the final analysis the general reader, even Caribbean readers, would tend to view the obeahman's prescriptions as a manifestation of syncretism.

Not only is *La paz del pueblo* imbued with the spirit of African religious philosophy, the *Samamfo* concept, as we have seen, but the work also displays the author's profound knowledge of christianity and indeed of the Bible. The main character, Pedro is effectively, albeit unwittingly, acknowledged by the pastor to be a Christ figure when the clergyman speaking for the pulpit applies to him the Biblical verse: " 'I will raise up one from among my people,' says the Lord, 'I will take away his heart of stone and give him a heart of flesh, and he will be the liberation of many and the glory of the people.' "[28] Pedro is also the special devotee of the African "god" "*cuminá*" (see note 20), who frequently possesses him. So he is an embodiment par excellence, of a process of syncretism.

[26] — Todas las noches ponés un balde de agua en el aptio. Luego te frotás con esto y te acostás —...

— Tenés que levantarte bien temprano todas las mañanas y regar la finca con el agua, siguiendo por los linderos que quendal al lado de Cristian...

— Y cuando vas a la finca vas a decir: "El Señor es grande y fuerte" siete veces (p. 79).

For an interesting treatment of the practice of obeah in contemporary Panama City, see Roy Simón Bryce-Laporte, "Religión folklórica y negros antillanos en la Zona del Canal de Panamá: Estudio de un incidente y su contexto," *Revista Nacional de Cultura*, No. 5 (Oct. Nov. Dic. 1976), pp. 61-80. Much of what Laporte says for Panama City applies to Limón, Costa Rica as well.

[27] This claim is made by the renowned Egyptologist Chiekh Anta Diop in *The African Origin of Civilization*. Trans. and ed. Mercer Cook (New York: Lawrence Hill, 1974), p. 6.

[28] "De entre mi pueblo levantaré a uno — dice el Señor — le quitaré el corazón de piedra y le daré uno do carne, y será la liberación de muchos y la gloria del pueblo" (p. 184).

Duncan's approach then to the religious theme is deeply symmetrical. For syncretism and antagonistic confrontation are the two polar extremes of the Costa Rican West Indian's response to the religious reality. Since religion is fundamental to the Afrocentric world view of these West Indians, the basic drama of their human condition is played out between these two poles. Duncan's artistic intuition has led him to this truth, which he is pleased to share with his readers.

By way of contrast, Cubena tends to minimize the religious factor in his portrayal of reality. Cubena himself was once a Catholic seminarian, just as Duncan was once, and perhaps still is, an Anglican priest. However, very little of Cubena's ecclesiastical experience is reflected in his works. He is thus a perfect foil to Duncan. Even so, the persistent religious centeredness of the West Indian folk philosophy surfaces from time to time in Cubena's universe. The protagonist of "La tercera ilusión," for example, is a homosexual tailor who is also a frequent smoker of marijuana. This leads some busybodies to the "obvious" conclusion: "In all doorways of El Chorrillo, wagging tongues asserted that the tailor's condition was the result of some *macuá* ("hex") put on him as a child" (my italics).[29]

In another story, "La familia," a desperate mother wrestling with the insurmountable problem of feeding her six fatherless children solicits the help of a "bruja penonomena" (a diviner from Penonomé), and then that of a "famosa santera cubana" (a famous Cuban obeahwoman). (Bryce Laporte in the article already mentioned in note 26 shows that this recourse to non-Christian religions is quite common during periods of crisis.) In Cubena's order of things the "hocuspocus" of the obeahpersons is basically impotent and of course ridiculous. The "santera cubana" prescribes a complicated and exotic remedy that sharply contrasts with the prescriptions of Mr. Sam, already discussed. Her remedy smacks of the stereotypic distortions invented by the detractors of Caribbean folk religious practices: "There she had to sacrifice three white doves, suck the blood from the heart of each one and take a special bath in urine mixed with yellow nance skins, green mango tree leaves, black buzzard feathers, wild boar fangs, dog hairs, iguana eggs..."[30] The woman finally resorts to the ritual immolation of her children and herself in order to bring forward the appointed time of their reunion with "Olodumare and the other happy ancestors in the Kingdom of the Dead."[31] This unnatural act of a woman driven beyond the brink of sanity represents Cubena's attempt to recreate an African mythology based not on the firmly held religious tenets of the West Indian folk, but rather on his book knowledge of African anthropology. In this instance, Cubena's inventive spirit leads him to a gratuitously distorted vision of the Caribbean world.

Cubena's recreation of African mythology in the quest of symbolic and soph-

---

[29] "En los zaguanes del Chorrillo, las malas lenguas afirmaban que la condición del sastre era el resultade de algún macúa que le habían echado cuando era niño" (p. 47).

[30] "Allá tuvo que sacrificar tres palomas blancas, chupar la sangre de cada corazón y tomarse un baño especial de orina mezclada con cáscaras amarillas de nance, hojas verdes del árbol de perro, huevos de iguana..." (p. 91).

[31] "Olodumare y los otros alegres antepasados en el Reino de los Muertos" (p. 93).

isticated Africanisms is much more successful in the story, "La abuelita africana." Here the author construct his narrative using Twi lexical items with the naturalness with which some speakers use Jamaican English words in their Spanish: "Un atardecer, una erubinrin (esclava) dio a luz a una omobinrin (hija) en el canaveral y escondió a la recién nacida..." (p. 78): At dusk one evening, an erubinrin (female slave) gave birth to an omobinrin (daughter) in the canefield and hid the newly born...). In this context the author freely introduces the religious theme: "She, from time to time, would implore Obatala, Yango and Ogun to give her strength to carry out her secret plan.'"[32] There are also references in this story to Odudua, Oshun, Yemaya, and other important symbols of African religiosity.

The same spirit of the artistic and artificial reconstruction of an African mythology is present in Duncan's short story, "Los mitos ancestrales." In this very interesting work from *La rebelión pocomía*, the main character is a personage from the *Samamfo*, who thus has the perfect vantage point for telling the history of African people. Duncan indeed has discovered an excellent artistic device, and has used it successfully in this story. This aspect of the religious theme is not, however, a direct reflection of the Caribbean folk tradition.

With regard to the theme of religion, Maloney's work is still too scant to provide any definitive trends. From what has been seen of Duncan's and even Cubena's work it should be clear that their use of the theme solidly establishes their ties with their Anglophone Caribbean background. This area of religion, as indeed too that of language, should be fertile field for future study.

Conclusion

The undeniable links with island culture were studied in the areas of language and religion. They could also be shown to exist in the areas of economics, dress, food, music and dance, and in physical appearance, among other areas. To state them is not merely to state the obvious, since they are generally ignored by people from the Caribbean islands, even the intellectuals. Furthermore, even the most cursory examination of the commonalities in Caribbean cultures leads the researcher to the concept of the African heritage.

This paper showed some of the obvious linguistic connections between a certain Panamanian and Costa Rican literature and that of the English-speaking Caribbean. (The latter literature alone has been considered by many to be the only "West Indian" literature. Unfortunately this misconception is quite widespread.) Such linguistic links are themselves consequences and indicators of a cultural experience shared by Africans transplanted to the Caribbean.

In the area of religion, the conflict and syncretism elements that this paper explored are, in general, common to all the folk religions of the Caribbean area. The function of African religiosity as a revolutionary force was also seen to be common. The paper also indicated similarities in some details: *pocomía* and Pukumina, for example. There are others that are just as obvious. One of them is the fact that Shango, the Yoruba ancestor is revered not only by Spanish-speaking

---

[32] "Ella, de tanto en tanto, imploraba a Obatalá, Yangó y Ogún que le dieran fuerza para llevar a cabo su sigiloso designio" (p. 79).

Yoruba Cubans and by English-speaking Yoruba Trinidadians but also by French-Creole-speaking Haitians who are mostly of Dahomean origin. Another such fact is the essential similarity in ritual and belief that exists between the Voodoo religion of the Haitians, the *santería* of the Cubans, the Kumina of the English-speaking Ashanti Jamaicans.

The signs of unity are too compelling to be ignored. Literature is one of the most fruitful media for the examination of the question of Caribbean cultural unity. This paper has entered into the question, which is also a quest. The conclusion suggested by the arguments and evidence presented is that a West Indian presence in the Hispanic works of prose and poetry produced by Carlos Guillermo Wilson, Gerardo Maloney, and Quince Duncan is paramount. Such a presence argues forcibly for the acceptance of the works by these authors as legitimate expressions of West Indian literature, to be duly included in the body of West Indian literature. This would indeed represent a significant development in West Indian literary criticism.

SARAH LEE: THE WOMAN TRAVELLER AND THE LITERATURE OF EMPIRE

Susan Greenstein
Western Washington University

The typical protagonist in the literature of Empire, whether in the boys' books of Henty, Buchan and Haggard, or in the "great tradition" of Conrad, Cary and Greene, goes to Africa to make a career, to make a fortune, to take his pleasure in the hunting of dangerous animals, or to pursue power in other forms. It is a given that the outsider uses Africa for his own purposes. Historically, as well as by literary convention, Africa is both opportunity and refuge, a stage for the enjoyment of special privilege and for the playing out of Western fantasies. As Raymond Williams puts it, during the nineteenth century Africa became the last place which can still serve as "the country" to complement an increasingly urban Britain.[1] With respect to the tradition of the country as an idyllic retreat based on economic exploitation that Williams is tracing, however, the African pastoral is distinguished by the ease with which any white man can achieve dominance, whether it is eagerly grasped or romantically declined. This fact is reflected in the literature of imperialism, whose central conventions and recurrent motifs interpret as a test of manhood, the encounter between a passive, if often malignant, continent, and the adventurers who penetrate it. The outcome is certain, since there is little real hindrance to their quests. In these romances and adventure tales, historical reality and cultural myths about the experiences men have are reinforced by one another.

White women may also achieve unprecedented freedom and easy authority in an African setting, especially if they are transients, rather than settlers. As travellers, the women become double adventurers, exploring more than new territory. In the early nineteenth century, when a Jane Austen heroine would be chastised by polite society for a brisk walk through muddy fields to visit a sick sister, Sarah Bowdich, later Sarah Lee, made three voyages to West Africa, several times travelling alone in rough trading ships. More important, she lived on her own at the coast for extended periods, dealing with local dignitaries and the exigencies of daily life with considerable spirit, while her first husband, T.E. Bowdich, negotiated a treaty with the Ashanti further inland.[2] At the end of the century, Mary Kingsley, freed from familial bondage by the death of her parents, "went down to West Africa to die" at the age of thirty-one, and found herself instead able to travel in uncharted and dangerous regions as a trader-naturalist, and to manage a host of carriers and servants, despite the extraordinary experience, for

[1] *The Country and the City* (New York: Oxford University Press, 1973), pp. 279-288.

[2] For biographical information on Sarah Lee, see *Gentleman's Magazine*, 201 (1856), 653-654, as well as her "Narrative" appended to T.E. Bowdich's *Excursions in Madeira and Porto Santo* (London: George B. Whittaker, 1925), pp. 200-218, and "Fragments from the Notes of a Traveller" in Sarah Lee's *Stories from Many Lands* (London: Moxon, 1835), pp. 251-362. The Notes to the stories themselves contain anecdotes from her African journeys.

these men, of working for a female.[3] She eventually became a significant influence on British "native policy." To the people they met, women like Sarah Lee and Mary Kingsley, especially if on their own, were simultaneously less than female (unhusbanded) and honorary males. In both fiction and non-fiction, other women, including contemporary anthropologists, have described the special prestige and peculiar limitations which marked their encounters with traditional African societies.[4]

The experiences of women in Africa cannot be adequately transcribed in the adventurers' vocabulary of the central tradition, yet most of those who write in the literature of Empire, like the men, do have first-hand knowledge of Africa. As a result, the conventions of the main tradition are often transformed or supplanted in their fiction. To suggest a few of these transformations: while women, too, may be found embellishing the myth of Africa as "heart of darkness" or archetypal female principle, they also provide the metaphor of the "garden which must be cultivated," and the figure of the "outsider as guest," as well demythologizing African geography and landscape and emphasizing an "anthropological" authenticity of detail in treating African societies. In addition to their unconventional experiences, to be in Africa at all women travellers had to free themselves from their own colonized situations, while female settlers responded to the influence of frontier life, which fostered a kind of independence less acceptable in England. These circumstances contributed strongly to the difference in point of view which distinguishes fiction by women within the larger tradition of an Africa as seen through Western eyes.

Sarah Lee was one of the first to write in what came to be the minor mode, with its discounting of marvels and tone of scientific inquiry. She wrote two novels and a series of stories set in West Africa, as well as children's tales. Among her contemporaries she was primarily known for her publications as a naturalist, but the fiction was also sought after. The stories were solicited for the Victorian "gift-book" annuals in the late 1820s and early 1830s when they were rapidly growing in popularity, and the more important of her West African novels, *The African Wanderers; or, the Adventures of Carlos and Antonio*, went through many editions on both sides of the Atlantic from its first appearance in 1847 through the end of the century.[5]

The African Wanderers combines the structure of the traveller's tale with that of the castaway (in later editions it was called *The African Crusoes*).[6] Two sailors, Carlos and Antonio (the first of whom is of gentle birth and breeding), are

[3] Quoted in Olwen Campbell, *Mary Kingsley: A Victorian in the Jungle* (London: Methuen, 1957), p. 43. The subtitle of this biography gives warning about its reliability beyond matters of fact.

[4] See Elenore Smith Bowen (pseud. for Laura Bohannan), *Return to Laughter: An Anthropological Novel* (New York: Harper, 1954), and Mariam K. Slater, *African Odyssey: An Anthropological Adventure* (Garden City, New York: Anchor, 1976).

[5] A number of the gift-book tales are collected in *Stories from Many Lands*. In her Introduction Sarah Lee explains the circumstances of their original publication.

[6] *The African Wanderers; or, The Adventures of Carlos and Antonio* (London: Griffith, Farran, Okeden & Welsh, 1889). This edition will be quoted in the text.

abandoned by their mutinous shipmates on an island somewhere in the Bight of Benin. Before their scarcely provisioned small boat breaks up, they make their way to the mainland in the region of Gabon. Moving inland, they travel from village to village, their friendly, extended stays in some places alternating with misadventures, including a period of enslavement in the court of a minor Muslim ruler. Eventually, with considerable assistance from their African hosts, they arrive at Cape Coast.

Sir Thomas; or, the Adventures of a Cornish Baronet in North-Western Africa (1856), is much thinner in its detailing of daily life among African peoples.[7] The story tells of the chastening of a family whose head refuses to acknowledge the terms on which Africa tolerates him. Sir Thomas, forced to abandon his land and castle by the plotting of an old enemy, sets out for West Africa with his son, daughter, servants, horses and hunting dogs, intending to redeem his pride and raise up a new inheritance for his children. They arrive, of course, not in the almost virgin territory they had been led to expect, but at a small settlement of British officials tenuously perched on the edge of the continent, existing in a carefully worked out arrangement with the Fanti and Ashanti rulers. Their instruction in the realities of West African life makes up the burden of the tale.

Many of the standard myths, stereotypes and ethnocentric attitudes that are so familiar in British writing on Africa appear in Sara Lee's work.[8] Yet the presiding spirit is one of careful observation and rational explanation. The scientific habit of mind, which leads her to provide Latin terminology and footnoted commentary for the flora and fauna that Carlos and Antonio come across, is pervasive. She and her protagonist in *The African Wanderers* also share a skeptical outlook: like Sarah Lee, Carlos takes every opportunity to discredit stories of fantastic creatures, as well as to correct more mundane biological misconceptions his less well-educated companion may have, and to gather accurate data.[9] Sarah Lee extends her reportorial bias to African societies, accompanying her short stories with notes almost as long again as the tales themselves, in order to provide the ethnographic material she is unable to fit into those brief fictions. While artless, this practice suggests the value she places on such anti-sensational information, and much of it turns up later, woven into the texts of her longer works. Geography is also treated factually: the wanderings of Carlos and Antonio can be shown to follow carefully what was

---

[7] *Sir Thomas; or, the Adventures of a Cornish Baronet in North-Western Africa* (London: Grant & Griffith, 1856). Also published as *Adventures in Fantiland* (London: Griffith, Farran, Okeden & Welsh, 1887) and in an American edition.

[8] The most comprehensive study of these conventions can be found in Dorothy Hammond and Alta Jablow, *The Myth of Africa* (New York: The Library of Social Science, 1877). See also G.D Killam *Africa in English Fiction, 1874-1939* (Ibadan, Nigeria: Ibadan University Press, 1968), and Philip D. Curtin, *The Image of Africa: British Ideas and Action, 1780-1850*, 2 vols. (Madison, Wisconsin; The University of Wisconsin Press, 1964).

[9] One must be careful to distinguish intention from execution. The best observer is subject to ethnocentric paradigms, at the very least, and the travellers of Sarah Lee's day, however openminded, were not aware of the complexity of cross-cultural studies. For example, like most "Europeans," Sarah Lee, and hence Carlos, exaggerate and misinterpret in their accounts of cannibalism. See Brian Weinstein, *Gabon: Nation-Building on the Ogooué* (Cambridge, Massachusetts: The M.I.T. Press, 1966), pp. 34-35 and p. 46 for a discussion of "cannibalism" among the Fang.

known of the territory through which they travelled, down to the names of small villages. The contrast with the later, "Rider Haggard" school of writing could not be greater. Haggard, who spent four years in government service in South Africa, considered it essential to spare the reader most of what he knew in the interest of the "grip" he wanted his romances to have.[10] Yet not only did he create landscapes in accord with his myth of Africa, he also followed the time-honored romancer's custom of supplying maps and other editorial paraphernalia to attest to the reality of his imaginary landscapes.

While Sarah Lee subscribes at times to national and racial stereotypes (applying them not only to blacks but to Irishmen, Scotsmen, and so forth), in practice the novel distinguishes with some care between different peoples and their ways of living. Carlos, for example, remarks on the indolence of Africans, offering the standard explanation of the natural abundance and tropical climate of the region, yet one of the major African characters (Wondo, of Naango, modelled on a man Sarah Lee met), compared the lack of enterprise of his compatriots unfavorably to the manufacturing skill of a neighboring people (AW, pp. 103 & 143). The full account questions Carlos' false generalization.

It does so because of Sarah Lee's practice of recording in detail everything Carlos and Antonio see or learn on their travels; just as in her stories she reports on numerous aspects of the African societies she encountered: marriages, funerals, religious ceremonies, foods, methods of cultivation, markets, clothes, medical practices, and the way names are given, among others. Though the product of an English sensibility, the stories are set within the Fanti world, with plots based on the lives of the African characters, rather than on the adventures of an outsider. While she does not observe these cultures as integrated wholes, the reader is nonetheless offered a view of a various landscape, with its seasonal transformations, and a portrait of peoples whose way of life is individual and dense. Even her strongest prejudices are open to question, if only through the inclusion of contradictory evidence. She speaks of the "Fetishman," for example, almost always to condemn the role of what we would call a witchdoctor, or less colorfully, an "ethnomedical practitioner," nor does it seem much of a concession when she compares the "Fetish" to European religious persecution, in the form of the Inquisition, especially since the latter is neither a British nor a contemporary evil. But on at least one occasion she shows the practice as a beneficial one, in a story concerned entirely with the fortunes of a Fanti protagonist.[11] Sarah Lee avoids both the anti-slavery advocates' usual strategy of finding the West African coast to be an earthly paradise and the later Conradian appropriation of Africa as a metaphor for Western decadence.

She does have affinities with writers from the era of the "enlightened traveller," whose influence lingered through her years in West Africa. The reasonable and dispassionate perspective of the eighteenth-century explorers' account acquires additional persuasiveness through the devices of her fictions.

---

[10] H. Rider Haggard, *The Days of My Life: An Autobiography* ed. C.J. Longman (London: Longman's, Green, 1926), II, 89 & 92. Haggard's landscapes are often realistic, but never at those key moments in the plot when the "essence of Africa" is suggested.

[11] "Agay, the Salt Carrier," *Stories from Many Lands*, pp. 152-179.

Particularly important in establishing the idea of Africa and of Africans in her novels are the frame stories about which her readers had little knowledge. In both of the African novels, the outsiders are petitioners, or uninvited guests, although Sir Thomas at first does not understand his position for what it is. Her main characters are placed by circumstance in dependent, almost helpless relation to the Africans they meet, in even greater measure than Sarah Lee herself was. *The African Wanderers*, in structure if not in spirit, might almost seem to foreshadow the Guinéan novelist Camara Laye's satire on the white adventurer in *The Radiance of the King*. His anti-hero, Clarence, is thrown up on the shores of West Africa, and loses himself in the depths of the continent, where, bewildered by cultures whose workings he is unable to comprehend, he is soon stripped of his notions of white superiority and self-sufficiency.[12] Carlos and Antonio do not share in the self-importance and overriding sense of mission which characterize most of the adventurers and explorers who people the literature of Empire, and certainly are free of the arrogance of the Henty hero, the "school-boy master of the world."[13]

Carlos, who is Sarah Lee's surrogate, is a dispossessed, British-educated Spaniard, true parentage unknown until the end of the novel, and his companion, a true Christian to all other men, but they recognize that they must rely on the good will, hospitality and guidance of the people they meet. Their helplessness is further underscored by their realization from the first that being white is no safeguard against being taken by slavers, as they eventually are. They return friendship without condescension, and honor all the obligations placed on them by the assistance they receive. When Carlos at last assumes his rightful station in the world, and also becomes a successful merchant, he sends gifts and, more significantly, business, the way of everyone who befriended him during his sojourn in West Africa.

Sarah Lee, who knew Arabic, trained as a naturalist along with her first husband, and after his early death devoted herself to the dissemination of what both had learned; nonetheless she found it best to write of her African adventures obliquely by giving many of them to a man, but one who is a "foreigner," compelled by his pride and warm temperament to leave the English household which had sheltered him. While Carlos seeks his fortune at sea, his more subdued older brother remains at home, with the family's full approval.

Olive Schreiner, Elspeth Huxley, and Margery Perham are among those who write more directly about the influence of the African experience on women of spirit, but share Sarah Lee's preference for celebrating the factual. Much of their politics and reporting, like hers, would not pass muster today. But their fiction does constitute an alternate tradition in the literature written by outsiders about Africa, and it is one which encourages observation by the light of common day.

[12] *The Radiance of the King* (1954, *Le regard du roi*; trans. New York: Collier Books, 1971).

[13] George Santayana, quoted in Killam, p. 19. For a catalogue of the attributes of the standard adventurers, see Roy Turnbaugh, "Images of Empire: George Alfred Henty and John Buchan," *Journal of Popular Culture*, 9 (1975), 434-440.